IMAGES
of Aviation

DALLAS/FORT WORTH
INTERNATIONAL
AIRPORT

IMAGES
of Aviation

DALLAS/FORT WORTH INTERNATIONAL AIRPORT

Bruce A. Bleakley

ARCADIA
PUBLISHING

Published by Arcadia Publishing
Charleston, South Carolina

Library of Congress Control Number: 2013941695

For all general information, please contact Arcadia Publishing:
Telephone 843-853-2070
Fax 843-853-0044
E-mail sales@arcadiapublishing.com
For customer service and orders:
Toll-Free 1-888-313-2665

Visit us on the Internet at www.arcadiapublishing.com

To Stacey

CONTENTS

ACKNOWLEDGMENTS

Most of the images in this book are courtesy of the Dallas/Fort Worth International Airport (D/FW), the History of Aviation Collection at the University of Texas at Dallas (UTD), the Frontiers of Flight Museum (FFM), and the C.R. Smith American Airlines Museum (CRS).

This book would not have been possible without a great deal of assistance from the staff of the Dallas/Fort Worth International Airport, who were all extremely generous with their time and expertise: David Magaña, senior manager of media relations; Harvey Holden, from the airport's Noise Compliance Office; Patrick Rinehart, Gary Wittman, and Donald Newport from Records Management; and Alan Black, director of the airport's Department of Public Safety, who hosted an exceptionally educational behind-the-scenes tour of one of the world's preeminent public safety organizations.

Former D/FW board member and chair Jan Collmer was an impeccable primary source of information for much of the airport's history. Joe M. Dealey Jr., the former director of public affairs, lent his support, knowledge, and guidance, and he introduced me to Len Limmer, D/FW's first chief of security, who provided valuable insights about the airport's first 25 years of operation.

Paul Oelkrug, Dr. Thomas Allen, and Patrizia Nava at the UTD's History of Aviation Collection graciously allowed me to peruse several extensive collections of material relating to the airport's history, and Tim McElroy of the C.R. Smith American Airlines Museum expertly guided me through the archives of D/FW's largest tenant.

At the Frontiers of Flight Museum, president and CEO Cheryl Sutterfield-Jones provided strong encouragement while also granting access to the archives; volunteers Mike Conlin and Randy Hinshaw helped with source materials and fact-checking; and former curator Col. Knox Bishop drew upon his encyclopedic knowledge of North Texas aviation history to provide a thorough review of the manuscript.

Aviation historian Don Pyeatt provided new sources and insights into the long Dallas–Fort Worth aviation rivalry from a Fort Worth point of view.

Finally, my sincere appreciation goes to my very patient acquisitions editor at Arcadia, Laura Bruns, for her guidance and support in navigating me through the various editorial deadlines.

INTRODUCTION

At the dedication of the airport halfway between Dallas and Fort Worth, speakers praised the cooperation of the two cities in the development of air activities in Texas, characterizing the site as "an ideal one to serve both Dallas and Fort Worth," and proclaiming that "there is glory enough for both Dallas and Fort Worth in the development of aeronautics in the Southwest."

It would be easy to assume those remarks were made at the opening of the Dallas/Fort Worth Regional (now International) Airport (D/FW) in January 1974. In fact, they were made in October 1929 at the dedication of the Curtiss-Wright Air Field, one of many fields that the Curtiss-Wright Company planned across the country to support its flying schools equipped with its airplanes. A proposal for joint use of the airfield by both cities failed to materialize, and such a cooperative spirit regarding a common airport would not surface again for 35 years.

In 1964, a federal mandate would force the issue, in what a local newspaper characterized as a "shotgun marriage." This paved the way for an airport 10 years later that would create a remarkable history in its first 40 years. As fascinating as the story of D/FW is, equally absorbing is the saga of the years leading up to the airport's opening day.

Dallas and Fort Worth were both founded in the mid-1800s in North Central Texas, a region lacking the seaport, navigable river, or major rail junction that formed the basis of the nation's largest cities. After the arrival of basic rail service in the 1870s, the two towns grew steadily, with Dallas always the larger of the two. A sometimes antagonistic rivalry developed as the towns competed for new railroad routes and associated industries. The competition would extend to aviation commerce in the next century.

By 1900, the Dallas–Fort Worth area was the largest population center in Texas, but it would be the new transportation conduit of aviation that would elevate the area to one of the largest metropolitan centers in the United States. In 1931, M.J. Norrell, manager of the Dallas Chamber of Commerce, prophetically stated to the Dallas Rotary Club, "As an inland city, let the air be our ocean, and let the influence of this city enlarge itself, carried on the wings of the planes that already write across our skies the story of a new era of transportation."

Both Dallas and Fort Worth were fortunate in having chamber of commerce organizations that believed early on in the potential of aviation. Indeed, the first airplane flights in Dallas (1910) and Fort Worth (1911) were the result of each chamber engaging professional aviators to perform exhibition flights. The chambers were also successful in petitioning the Army to establish flight-training airfields near their respective cities in support of the military buildup in World War I.

In the years following the war, the Army's Love Field became Dallas's municipal airport, while Fort Worth used the Army's Barron Field for a short time before establishing what would become Meacham Field closer to town. When the Kelly Act of 1925 replaced the postal service's airmail flight operations with contracts to commercial carriers, the two cities vigorously competed for those operations and the commercial airlines that grew from them.

Throughout the 1930s, both Meacham and Love Fields were improved and expanded to meet a growing commercial aviation industry. Dallas's airfield consistently handled more traffic, due the city's larger population. The idea of a common airport to serve both cities surfaced again in 1940, when the Civil Aeronautics Board (CAB) suggested it in response to both cities' funding requests for their respective airports.

Negotiations for a proposed "Midway Airport" reflected the long-standing rivalry between the two municipalities. Talks became contentious with respect to details, and Dallas leaders bowed out of the project. Nevertheless, Midway's runway system was built and used for military training during World War II. After the war, the site became attractive to Fort Worth leaders as they realized that Meacham Field could not be expanded to meet an unprecedented postwar demand for commercial aviation.

Largely through the efforts of influential businessman Amon G. Carter, Midway was annexed by Fort Worth as the Greater Fort Worth International Airport in 1947, with the secondary (but more widely used) name of Amon G. Carter Field added during the 1950 ground-breaking ceremony for a terminal building. Beginning flight operations in 1953, the new airport never attracted the commercial air traffic its planners anticipated, and after the initial bloom of opening day, its flight operations began to decline as Love Field's passenger count rose.

For its part, the federal government was becoming more reluctant to provide improvement funds for two large commercial airports only 12 air miles apart. The 1964 mandate requiring the two cities to agree on a common airport had a moderating effect on their once bitter rivalry. The cities' representatives were surprisingly quick to create an amicable working relationship, acknowledging that neither of the current airports would have the capacity to meet the area's future commercial aviation needs.

The result of that mandate, the Dallas/Fort Worth International Airport, has the largest operational capacity of any airport in the world, due to the foresight of its planners. With over 260,000 jobs and billions of dollars of development directly or indirectly tied to D/FW, it has also been a phenomenal catalyst for the area. From the beginning, the airport was envisioned as not only a commercial aviation center, but also a major driver of the area's economic growth.

One

COMMERCIAL AVIATION
COMES TO NORTH TEXAS

On May 12, 1926, National Air Transport began the first regularly scheduled commercial air service in the state of Texas, flying the mail out of Dallas's Love Field and Fort Worth's Meacham Field before heading north to Chicago. In one of the first clashes of their decades-long aviation rivalry, Dallas and Fort Worth each lobbied aggressively to have its airport designated as the southern terminus of the route.

By 1930, proposals had been made regarding a common regional airfield between the two cities, but for the time being, each city concentrated on developing its respective airport. In 1940, the Civil Aeronautics Board (CAB) suggested that money could be available for a joint airport project. The cities initially participated in plans to develop the Midway Airport equidistant between them, but before a terminal building was constructed, differences of opinion caused Dallas leaders to withdraw from the project. The facility's runways were built, but were used only for military training during World War II.

After the war, the City of Fort Worth began to develop the Midway site, not only as a replacement for Meacham Field, but also in hopes of convincing federal officials and the airlines of the site's potential as the region's single commercial aviation facility. Under the strong leadership of Fort Worth businessman and newspaper publisher Amon G. Carter, the new airport opened in 1953.

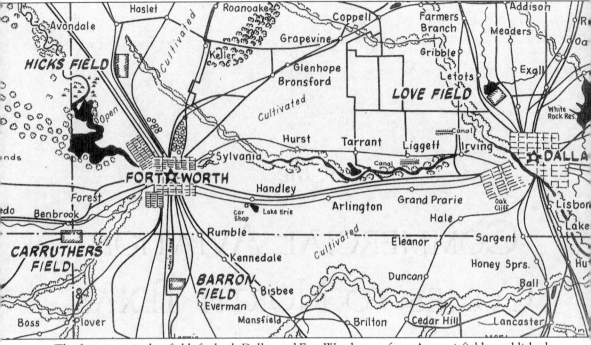

The first municipal airfields for both Dallas and Fort Worth grew from Army airfields established to train aviators during World War I. This 1918 map segment shows Love Field northwest of Dallas and the three Army fields around Fort Worth—Hicks to the northwest, Carruthers to the southwest, and Barron to the south. After the war, the Army left Love, Hicks, and Carruthers, but kept Barron Field as a surplus depot. In the early 1920s, the federal government established the Model Airways System, a network of airfields and routes to facilitate the development of air commerce and military aviation transport capability. Both Love and Barron Fields would become stops for postal service airmail planes as part of that system. Barron would also become Fort Worth's first municipal flying field, but only for a short time. A half-century after this map was drawn, ground breaking for the Dallas/Fort Worth Regional Airport would take place in the large open area south of the town of Grapevine (top center). (FFM.)

When the Army left Love Field at the end of World War I, the chamber of commerce retained ownership of the facility and leased it back to the city as a municipal airport. Gradually, the Army hangars and other facilities became populated with operators, often former Army pilots with Army surplus planes, who provided flying lessons, rides, aircraft sales, fuel, maintenance, and other aviation services. (FFM.)

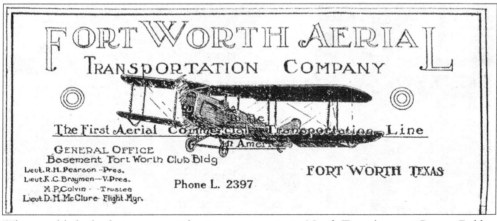

What was likely the first commercial aviation enterprise in North Texas began at Barron Field in 1919. A group of former Army aviators (listed in this newspaper advertisement) formed the Fort Worth Aerial Transportation Company, using surplus Curtiss JN-4 "Jennies" to carry passengers and small loads of freight to locations in Oklahoma and North Texas. The service operated only a few months before going out of business. (*Fort Worth Star-Telegram.*)

In 1923, the Army offered to keep Barron Field (shown here in 1918) as part of the Model Airways System if Fort Worth would maintain it as a municipal airport. The Fort Worth Chamber of Commerce provided funds to improve the field in 1924, and, although it was several miles south of the city via unimproved roads, Barron became Fort Worth's first municipal flying field. (US Army via Don Pyeatt.)

Due to difficulties involved in maintaining the airport, the Army decided to close Barron Field in 1925. It sent SSgt. W.G. Fuller (right, with a Lieutenant Cole) to begin packing up equipment and closing the facility. Faced with the prospect of losing its flying field, Fort Worth negotiated with the Army to reestablish a Model Airways airmail stop at a closer airfield being planned north of downtown. (FFM.)

Mayor H.C. Meacham lobbied strongly with the Army to keep Fort Worth on the Model Airways System at its new airfield. He also asked to have Sergeant Fuller assigned to manage the Army operations at the new field, pledging his own money to build a caretaker's cottage and dig a well. (City of Fort Worth via Don Pyeatt.)

First established as the Fort Worth Municipal Airport, the new airfield north of town was renamed Meacham Field in 1927 in honor of H.C. Meacham, the former Fort Worth mayor who was instrumental in its inception. W.G. Fuller, now a civilian, was hired as the airfield manager, beginning an aviation career in Fort Worth that would last almost 40 years. (CRS.)

The Air Mail Act of 1925 phased out the postal service's airmail flight operations and authorized Postmaster General Harry S. New to award the routes to commercial carriers. Chicago's National Air Transport (NAT) was awarded the route between Chicago and the Dallas–Fort Worth area, and both Texas cities lobbied to be the route's southern terminus. (Library of Congress.)

Airmail service to and from the Dallas–Fort Worth area was a highly anticipated event. This newspaper invitation to a dedication ceremony at Dallas's Love Field on August 6, 1926, shows the route that mail planes would follow, from Dallas through Fort Worth (hidden behind the fold on left) and then northward to Chicago to join the transcontinental route to New York. (*Dallas Morning News*.)

On May 12, 1926 the First Air Mail Will Come to Dallas Bringing New York and Chicago 48 Hours Nearer

Attend the Air Mail Carnival This Afternoon

Celebrations leading up to the beginning of air mail service included dedication ceremonies for two of NAT's boxy but dependable Curtiss "Carrier Pigeon" aircraft, shown here as rendered by artist Nixon Galloway. *Miss Dallas* and *Miss Fort Worth* were dedicated at Love Field on May 6, and at Meacham Field on May 8, 1926, respectively. (FFM.)

NAT pilot Herb Kindred, shown here in a later photograph, piloted the first airmail flight out of Love Field on May 12, 1926. He would also fly NAT's first passenger flight out of Love Field in 1927 and the first night airmail flight in 1928. (UTD.)

Local department stores quickly took advantage of the airmail service, advertising the availability of men's and women's clothing and accessories just arrived from "the fashion centers of the east." Some stores had even placed advertisements for goods arriving by airmail before the service began. (*Dallas Morning News.*)

On September 1, 1927, NAT added passenger service on the route to and from Chicago via the enclosed-cabin Travel Air Model 5000 aircraft. The plane could carry, in addition to the mail, up to three passengers in relatively comfortable wicker seats. Seat belts were optional. The one-way fare to Chicago was $100.30; the fare to Fort Worth was $3.50. (San Diego Air & Space Museum.)

On February 6, 1928, Texas Air Transport (TAT) began flying the mail between Dallas and cities in South Texas. The airline was owned by Fort Worth bus line owner Temple Bowen. At a dedication ceremony the day before, Bowen's fleet of Pitcairn Mailwing aircraft (one of which is shown here with an unidentified pilot) was christened by influential Fort Worth newspaper publisher and businessman Amon G. Carter, who was rapidly becoming a prominent voice for Fort Worth's aviation endeavors. (FFM.)

Amon G. Carter was one of the investors who backed Fort Worth businessman A.P. Barrett in buying Bowen's interest in TAT in October 1928. Barrett expanded the operation and changed its name to Southern Air Transport, which became a predecessor company of American Airways (later American Airlines). Consequently, Carter became American's major stockholder, a position he would leverage whenever possible to Fort Worth's advantage in its commercial aviation rivalry with Dallas. (Library of Congress.)

In 1929, the Curtiss-Wright Company acquired a site for Curtiss-Wright Air Field, outlined at lower left in the photograph above. The site, just southwest of Grand Prairie (center), was to be used for another of the company's flying schools. Seen in the image below, the ground-breaking ceremony on October 30, 1929, featured an airplane with Fort Worth Association of Commerce member Jack Hott pulling a plow wielded by Dallas mayor J. Waddy Tate. In a cooperative spirit that would not be repeated for many years, speakers characterized the airfield, slightly closer to Dallas than Fort Worth, as ideal to serve both cities. The Dallas Chamber of Commerce proposed to Fort Worth that the airfield become the single airport for both cities' airmail service, offering to give up Love Field as an airmail stop. In June 1930, Fort Worth declined the offer, and each city continued to improve its respective airport through the 1930s. (Above, FFM; below, *Dallas Morning News*.)

Plane Pulls Plow in Ground Breaking at Airport

By the early to mid-1930s, Dallas's Love Field was gaining a reputation as one of the nation's best airports. The large grass landing area had given way to paved runways, and modern terminal buildings and hangars replaced many of the Army structures built during World War I. One of the firms serving both Love Field and Fort Worth's Meacham Field at the time was Bowen Airlines, which was operating the speedy eight-passenger Lockheed Orion, as depicted in the ad detail below. The plane could cruise at 180 miles per hour, making the straight-line trip between the two airports in less than 10 minutes. (Both, FFM.)

19

Largely through the efforts of Amon G. Carter, Meacham Field opened a new $150,000 air-conditioned terminal building in 1937. The terminal was dedicated to Carter, and superlatives were heaped upon him by the dedication speakers—indications of his influence in aviation matters. Above, a Lockheed Electra and Douglas DC-2s from American, Delta, and Braniff represent the three major airlines serving both Meacham Field and Dallas's Love Field, 25 miles to the east, in the late 1930s. The 14-passenger DC-2 and the 21-passenger DC-3 shown below at the Meacham terminal, with their greater speed, range, and capacity, represented commercial aviation progress. These advancements, however, made it less feasible for the planes to serve two airports only 25 miles apart—a fact not lost on the airlines that were flying them. (Both, UTD.)

Not to be outdone, in October 1940, the City of Dallas dedicated a new $225,000 air-conditioned terminal building for Love Field (pictured). Located on Lemmon Avenue, at the east side of the airport, the building was larger than Meacham Field's terminal. Also in 1940, the idea of a common airport for both cities surfaced again when the Civil Aeronautics Board (CAB), responding to funding requests from both Love and Meacham Fields, offered to provide federal aid if the cities would agree on a joint airport. Contemporary newspaper reports indicate that both Dallas and Fort Worth agreed on the concept of a Midway Airport, but only as an airport for "national defense" while the cities' two airports kept their respective commercial air traffic. In mid-October 1941, as the country seemed more destined to be drawn into World War II, an agreement was finally reached to build the facility, first for the immediate military need and later to serve as a commercial airport, operated by Dallas, Fort Worth, the small town of Arlington, American Airlines, and Braniff. (Will Blunt.)

Just over a year after Love Field's new terminal building was dedicated, the United States entered World War II, and the airport soon became the home of the Air Transport Command's 5th Ferrying Group. This generated a rapid buildup of the airfield's infrastructure, mostly on the south side of the airport, as shown in this northwest-looking view. Lockheed Aircraft Company established a modification facility (the large hangars at lower right) for both bomber and fighter aircraft. Between those two operations, air traffic at Love Field increased dramatically. Over 100 aircraft are visible in the photograph. The new facilities built to support these operations, as well as the experience gained from managing the resulting heavy air traffic, would prove valuable after the war as Love expanded to meet the rising demand in commercial aviation. The new terminal building can be seen along Lemmon Avenue at upper right. (FFM.)

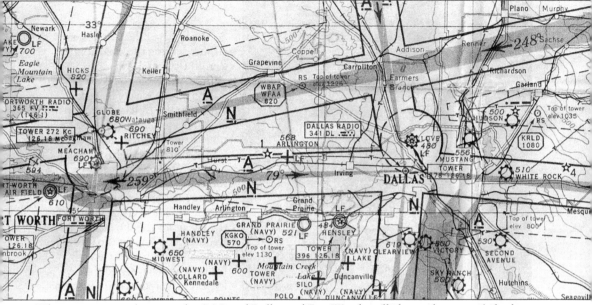

When negotiations between the CAB and Dallas and Fort Worth stalled over the issue of whether the Midway Airport would be used for commercial air traffic, the small town of Arlington (just below center in this aeronautical chart) stepped in to propose operating the airport in partnership with American Airlines and Braniff. This development quickly brought Dallas and Fort Worth back to the bargaining table, resulting in an October 1941 agreement wherein Dallas, Fort Worth, Arlington, and the two airlines would form a Midway Airport Corporation to administer the airport. The terminal building would be on the north side of the field on State Highway 183, equidistant from the downtown areas of Dallas and Fort Worth. The CAB would commission a plan for the airport, but in the meantime, the runways were built and used for military training. The airfield's location is identified as "ARLINGTON" in the center of this chart. A cross symbol indicates its use as a military training field. (FFM.)

As the heads of the two largest airlines serving the area, Tom Braniff (left) and American Airlines' C.R. Smith (below) welcomed the idea of a single airport in the Dallas–Fort Worth area. This would simplify their route structures; regional and transcontinental flights would need to make only one stop between the two cities. As planning for the Midway Airport progressed, an engineering firm engaged to design the layout for the site placed the terminal building on the west side of the field, facing Fort Worth. Dallas leaders protested the new location vigorously, suspecting that Amon G. Carter had influenced the change. The resulting enmity, which would not subside for over two decades, led Dallas to withdraw from the Midway Airport project in 1943. (Both, UTD.)

After World War II, the 44-passenger capacity of the Douglas DC-4 more than doubled that of the popular DC-3, introduced 10 years earlier. The DC-6, like the Delta aircraft seen here at Love Field, with even greater capacity, would not be able to operate fully loaded out of Meacham Field without significant airport improvements. This caused Fort Worth officials to rethink the city's airport options. (FFM.)

Faced with Meacham Field's limitations, the City of Fort Worth began developing the Midway Airport, not only as a replacement for Meacham, but, hopefully, as the region's designated commercial airport. This southwest-looking view shows the new terminal building under construction, in the west side location that Dallas had found objectionable. It is difficult to imagine how the terminal could be located to the north, given the location of State Highway 183 (lower right). (UTD.)

It was believed that a newer and larger facility than Love Field, located at the Midway Airport site, would appeal to both the airlines and the CAB. Amon Carter and other Fort Worth officials had quietly negotiated with them to develop the site. When the announcement was made in 1947 that the Greater Fort Worth International Airport would be developed as a commercial airport, Dallas officials were initially concerned about its effect on the traffic at Love Field. However, events would prove that the new airport would not take as much air traffic from Love as they initially feared. The airport was dedicated with the additional name Amon G. Carter Field, after the man who was most responsible for its creation, during ground-breaking ceremonies for the terminal in 1950. The airport began flight operations in April 1953. American Airlines president C.R. Smith had unsuccessfully urged Carter, his major stockholder, not to accept the honor of having his name on the airport, believing it would hamper efforts to re-engage Dallas in the facility's operation. (CRS.)

Two

THE RIVALRY INTENSIFIES

Now that Amon G. Carter Field, with its greatly increased capacity over Meacham Field, was in operation, competition in commercial aviation between Dallas and Fort Worth became more intense. Fort Worth now had an airport that could easily accommodate a fully loaded DC-6, the follow-on DC-7, and the proposed jet airliners being developed. (The Boeing 367-80, the prototype for the famous 707, would make its first flight the year after Carter Field's dedication.)

Leaders in both Dallas and Fort Worth, realizing that transcontinental flights would make only one stop while traversing the country, were eager to show that their respective facility was the best choice. This led to Love and Carter Fields operating in parallel long after it was practical to do so. Airlines traversing the country grudgingly flew the short hop between the two airports; by 1962, some 10,000 flights a year were making this uneconomical 12-mile trip.

Fort Worth's new airport was never able to garner the volume of air traffic hoped for by Amon G. Carter and other local leaders. It consistently operated at a deficit (the average cost per enplaned passenger at Carter Field was over $40, while at Love Field, the figure was just over $5). As the 1950s progressed, airline traffic at Carter Field declined while Love's continued to grow. For their part, the airlines were simply operating flights where the passengers were.

Fort Worth made overtures to Dallas more than once to participate in the former's airport operation, but Dallas leaders firmly declined, citing the fact that the majority of the region's airline passengers came from Dallas. Those passengers would be inconvenienced by having to use "the 19-Mile Airport," a reference to the driving distance to Amon G. Carter Field for most Dallasites.

In the early 1960s, Fort Worth again petitioned the federal government to specify a single regional airport, with the obvious hope that the centrally located Carter Field would be the choice. Federal officials declined to designate either Love Field or Amon G. Carter Field as the area's regional facility, but in September 1964, the Civil Aeronautics Board rendered an ultimatum by requiring the two cities themselves to agree on a common airport. The stage was set for Dallas and Forth Worth to finally cooperate on what would become one of the most remarkable airport projects in aviation history.

Fort Worth's 1,780-acre Amon G. Carter Field was a great improvement over Meacham Field, and it boasted more space than Dallas's 600-acre Love Field. In this photograph, taken shortly after the airport began operations, airplanes are lined up at most of the terminal's 17 gates. (Love Field had 12 gates.) (CRS.)

The 240,000-square-foot terminal at Amon G. Carter Field was significantly larger than Love Field's 1940 building. Appointed with Western art and furnishings, the main lobby was declared by one aviation writer as "the finest in the world." However, as airline traffic at Carter declined while Love's increased, a crowded terminal, as seen here, would occur less frequently. (UTD.)

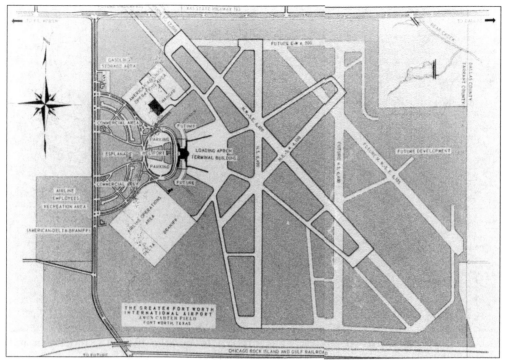

The most obvious barriers to expanding Amon G. Carter Field were the railroad right-of-way on the south airfield boundary and a major highway (State 183) on the north. This map indicates the planners' intent to lengthen the northwest-southeast runway over Highway 183 to accommodate the proposed jet airliners then being designed. In fact, the north-south runway was later lengthened, with a tunnel underneath to accommodate the highway. (UTD.)

While Dallas's Love Field was capable of handling a fully loaded DC-6 and the newer 74-passenger DC-7, the terminal facilities were stretched to the limit to accommodate a continually expanding postwar demand for air travel. Extensions to the original 1940 terminal building stretching to the north and east (shown here) were proving inadequate by the early 1950s, and planning had begun for a new and larger terminal building. (FFM.)

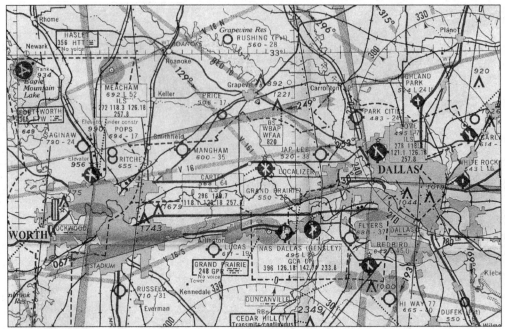

As Dallas and Fort Worth operated separate airports through the 1950s, the functional and economic impracticality of the situation became increasingly obvious. The 1957 aeronautical chart (above) shows the large metropolitan areas of Fort Worth on the left and Dallas on the right. Amon G. Carter Field is in the center (represented by the dark circle with three crossed runways), only 12 air miles from Love Field (just above the *D* in the name Dallas). The far right column of a 1955 Braniff timetable (below) shows Flight 300 leaving Dallas Love Field at 5:40 p.m. and arriving at Fort Worth's Amon Carter Field at 5:55, before departing for Amarillo. Of the 15 minutes on the schedule, less than half were in the air; it is unlikely the twin-engine Convair reached its regular cruising speed. (Both, FFM.)

	"	Lv		▼
Dallas	"	Ar		5 12
	"	·Lv		5 40
Fort Worth ¶	"	Ar		5 55
	"	Lv		* 6 10
TEXARKANA	"	Lv	↓	To
FT. SMITH	" {	Ar	2 50	Ama-
	" {	Lv	3 00	rillo
Oklahoma City	"	Ar		See
	"	Lv	↓	Page
				7
Tulsa	"	Ar	3 45	
	"	Lv	4 00	**Convair**
Wichita	"	Ar		**300**
	"	Lv		

As operations at Love Field expanded through the 1950s, traffic at Amon Carter Field continued to decline. However, in 1957, American Airlines opened its new Stewardess College, the world's first facility devoted specifically to flight-attendant training, just west of the airport. The building, shown with a graduating class in this perfectly timed and unretouched photograph, is still used for the same purpose. (CRS.)

To replace the overcrowded 1940 terminal building on Lemmon Avenue, Love Field in January 1958 opened a new terminal in the center of the airport that was half again as large as the one at Amon G. Carter Field. This photograph illustrates the dramatic technological changes taking place in commercial aviation at the time, with three piston-engine DC-7s in the foreground and four new Boeing 707 jetliners at the opposite concourse. (CRS.)

By 1960, jet airliners such as the Boeing 707 were a reality. Lady Bird Johnson, wife of Sen. Lyndon B. Johnson (D-Texas), is shown here with American Airlines executive Otto Becker inaugurating the first jet service out of Dallas Love Field on July 12, 1959. The Dallas and Fort Worth airports were able to accommodate the 707 and other jetliners, but as civic leaders continued to promote their respective facilities, they were privately having doubts about either airport's ability to accommodate coming advances in commercial aircraft technology. (CRS.)

In the early 1960s, supersonic transports and the Boeing 747 "jumbo jet" (shown here) were on the drawing boards, and there were indications that neither Love Field nor Amon Carter Field would be able to expand to accommodate these aircraft at their full capabilities. (FFM.)

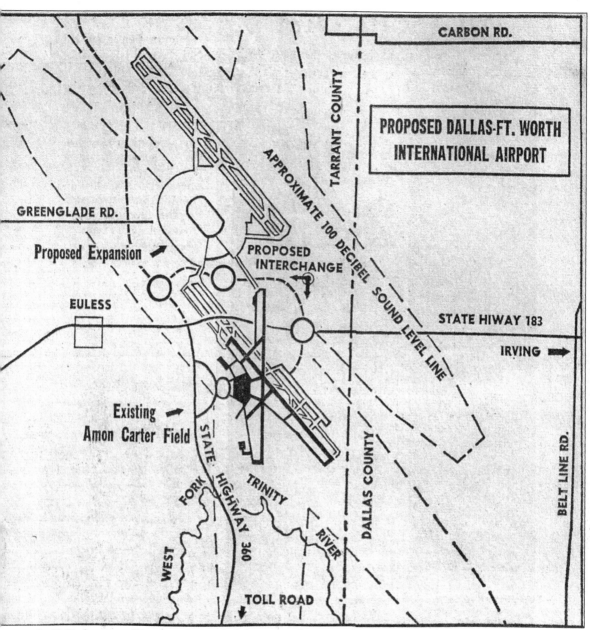

In 1962, the City of Fort Worth changed the name of its airport to Greater Southwest International Airport—Dallas–Fort Worth Airfield. Hoping to save its investment in the airport, the city appealed to the Civil Aeronautics Board (CAB) to designate it as the regional facility for the area. The name change was also supposedly made to appeal again to Dallas to join in the airport's operation. The change, however, had the opposite effect. The airport was then renamed once again, to simply Greater Southwest International Airport (GSIA); it continued to be referred to locally as Amon G. Carter Field. This drawing, published in the *Dallas Morning News* with even another proposed name, was an attempt to show how the airport could be expanded to serve as the region's primary airport, capable of handling a rapidly growing demand for air travel and the new aircraft that would serve that demand. (FFM.)

Also in 1962, Federal Aviation Administration (FAA) chief Najeeb Halaby declared that no more funds would be available for Love Field improvements as long as a good jetport (GSIA) was available nearby. In response to Fort Worth's request, the CAB ordered hearings to address the issue of a single airport for Dallas and Fort Worth, which began in spring 1963 and were chaired by CAB examiner Ross Newmann. (UTD.)

This northward-looking view of Love Field shows the obstacles to expansion that concerned FAA administrator Najeeb Halaby. He was convinced that Bachman Lake to the northwest (at extreme left center) and the surrounding commercial and residential development made it impractical to expand the airport to accommodate bigger jet airliners. (FFM.)

- iii -

UNITED STATES OF AMERICA
CIVIL AERONAUTICS BOARD
WASHINGTON, D. C.

DALLAS-FORT WORTH REGIONAL AIRPORT INVESTIGATION

DOCKET 13959

It would not be in the public interest to designate at this time either GSIA or Love Field as a regional airport to serve the Dallas-Fort Worth area.

This investigation is terminated.

In a startlingly brief and terse statement at the beginning of his 50-page final report dated April 7, 1964, CAB examiner Newmann declined to designate either city's airport as the primary facility for the Dallas–Fort Worth region. He criticized both cities and their airports for facility limitations and duplication of efforts, while outlining his basic requirements for a common airport. He also recommended the creation of a joint airport authority, free of civic bias, to cooperate in good faith in planning and building a shared airport in the best possible location. Fort Worth was especially dissatisfied with the "non-decision," as its officials put it, and asked the full board to review Newmann's ruling. Both cities presented their arguments—again—and on September 30 the board issued a surprise ruling. Newmann's decision was allowed to stand, but an additional ruling required that Dallas and Fort Worth would have to be served by a common airport. They had 180 days to agree to do so, or the board would decide the matter for them. (UTD.)

Suddenly, the years of acrimonious debate and competition were over. In short order, Dallas and Fort Worth each selected three representatives to arrive at an initial agreement within the CAB's 180-day deadline. Key players among these negotiators, who began meeting in closed session, were J. Erik Jonsson, the new mayor of Dallas (left), and J. Lee Johnson III, chairman of the Fort Worth chamber's aviation board (below). By May 1965, the group had produced a memorandum of understanding for the respective city councils. Beginning the work of making the new airport a reality, they began looking for a suitable architectural firm for the vast project. The team of "Jonsson & Johnson" took the lead in this effort, and in July 1965, selected the firm Tippets-Abbett-McCarthy-Stratton (TAMS) Engineers and Architects of New York. (Left, UTD; below, FFM.)

The first task for TAMS was the selection of a site an equal distance from both Dallas and Fort Worth and suitable for a large airport with room to expand. The chosen site, announced in September 1965, was just north of the existing Greater Southwest International Airport (GSIA), the northern part of which can be seen at the bottom of this image. Outlines of the five north-south runways and two northwest-southeast runways are superimposed on the aerial photograph. Road access was a major consideration in the selection of the site, located just south of State Highway 114 (top) and north of State Highway 183 (bottom). Initial considerations called for the acquisition of 5,000 or 6,000 acres, but the final figure recommended by the planners was a staggering 18,000 acres—10 times the size of GSIA. (UTD.)

Boeing's proposal for a supersonic transport was the Model 733 (later known as the 2707), shown here with its variable-sweep wings extended for takeoff in a 1964 company rendering. Projected to compete with the British/French Concorde then in development, it was cancelled for financial and environmental reasons. However, advanced designs such as this and the Boeing 747 were clearly in the minds of the D/FW planners. (FFM.)

The Boeing 747 was one of the most highly anticipated aircraft in commercial aviation history. Able to carry 450 passengers or more in a high-density seating configuration, it caused D/FW's planners to consider ways to load and off-load large numbers of passengers, including this proposal that would have involved four terminal gates supporting four separate jetways. Experience proved, however, that one jetway, as used to this day at D/FW, was sufficient. (CRS.)

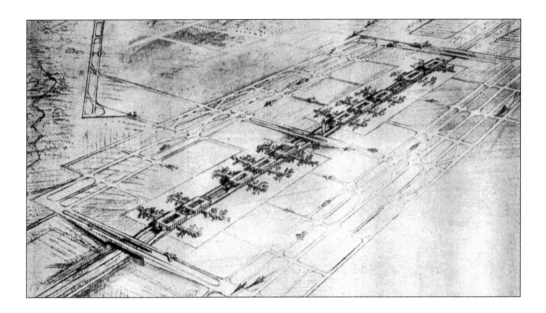

From the start, TAMS architects recognized that the new airport would have to accommodate large numbers of passengers, based on the nation's rapid growth in air travel. They envisioned a terminal complex that would consist of a series of rectangular sub-terminals along a "spine" roadway running underneath the sub-terminals and parallel to the runways and taxiways on either side (above). Passengers could be picked up or dropped off from the roadway at their specific sub-terminals, a relatively short distance from their gates. For passengers parking their cars at the airport, spiral ramps at each sub-terminal would lead to upper-level parking decks, allowing access into the building by elevator or escalator. The diagram below shows the layout of some of the sub-terminals, with a varying number of gates depending on aircraft size. (Both, CRS.)

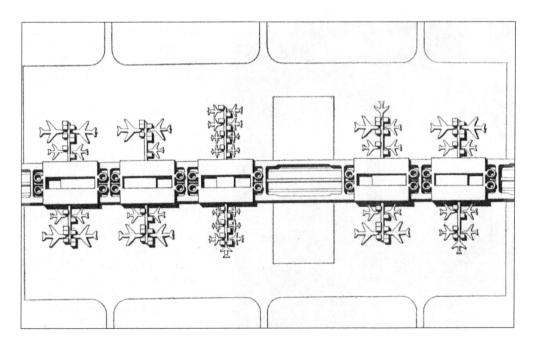

Early on, Thomas Sullivan, the airport's first executive director, was concerned about the terminal design proposed by TAMS, believing it represented a present-day approach to a totally new situation. In particular, he was concerned that a conventional terminal layout could be quickly saturated by the hundreds of passengers from two or more of the anticipated wide-body jetliners, such as the Boeing 747. (D/FW.)

To further define the airport plan, Sullivan hired two noted airport architects: Gyo Obata (shown here) of the St. Louis firm Hellmuth, Obata, & Kassabaum (HOK); and Richard Adler of New York's Brodsky, Hopf, and Adler. Obata was lead for the project. He envisioned a decentralized approach, with smaller individual terminals on a more "human" scale. Emphasis was placed on how easy it would be for a person to operate within the building. (HOK.)

Instead of the elongated complex of sub-terminals originally proposed by TAMS, Obata envisioned a series of semicircular structures, as shown in one of his original sketches (above). The semicircular construction allowed more space for aircraft parked about the outer perimeter, including the anticipated wide-body jets that had prompted Sullivan to consider reviewing the original plan. It also featured parking on the inside of each semicircle, resulting in a relatively short walk from a passenger's car to the boarding gate. The wisdom of Obata's approach was validated when the airport began operations. In the photograph below, several jetliners, including two Boeing 747s, are arranged around the outer perimeter of one of the terminals. (Above, HOK; below, HOK photograph by George Silk.)

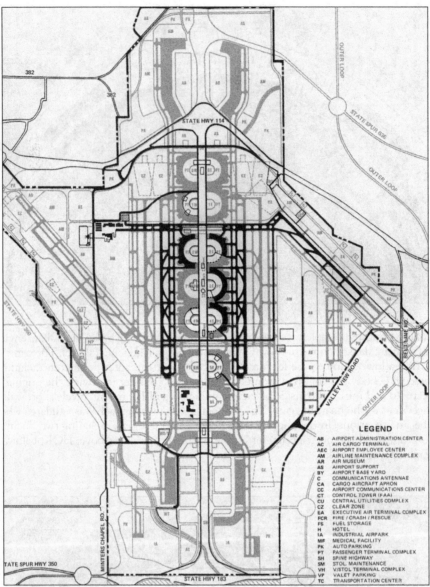

LEGEND

AB	AIRPORT ADMINISTRATION CENTER
AC	AIR CARGO TERMINAL
AEC	AIRPORT EMPLOYEE CENTER
AM	AIRLINE MAINTENANCE COMPLEX
AR	AIR MUSEUM
AS	AIRPORT SUPPORT
BY	AIRPORT BASE YARD
C	COMMUNICATIONS ANTENNAE
CA	CARGO AIRCRAFT APRON
CC	AIRPORT COMMUNICATIONS CENTER
CT	CONTROL TOWER (FAA)
CU	CENTRAL UTILITIES COMPLEX
CZ	CLEAR ZONE
EA	EXECUTIVE AIR TERMINAL COMPLEX
FCR	FIRE / CRASH / RESCUE
FS	FUEL STORAGE
H	HOTEL
IA	INDUSTRIAL AIRPARK
MF	MEDICAL FACILITY
PK	AUTO PARKING
PT	PASSENGER TERMINAL COMPLEX
SH	SPINE HIGHWAY
SM	STOL MAINTENANCE
VH	V/STOL TERMINAL COMPLEX
VP	VALET PARKING
TC	TRANSPORTATION CENTER

The result of Gyo Obata's reworking of the original TAMS terminal design was a master plan featuring up to 13 individual semicircular terminals, retaining the central north-south thoroughfare of the airport, the International Parkway, and localized parking at individual terminals. The decentralization achieved through individual terminals would allow for future expansion with the least disruption to existing operations, and the parking configuration for each terminal would allow those arriving by car to reach their gates by walking an average distance of 300 feet. When executive director Sullivan presented the proposed design change, the airport board initially expressed concern that the change might jeopardize the projected 1972 opening date. However, Obata and his team completed the plan details in eight intense weeks, and the change was approved. For the initial construction phase, four terminals would be built (indicated in this image by darker shading), along with the first three runways and supporting taxiways. The terminals were initially designated 2W (for "west"), 2E ("east"), 3E, and 4E. (UTD.)

One of the parcels of land on the proposed airport property was the site of Minter's Chapel, a Methodist church that had been established in the 1850s. In 1967, the airport acquired the land, except for the cemetery, and the church was relocated. The cemetery remains on the west side of the airport to this day. (Author.)

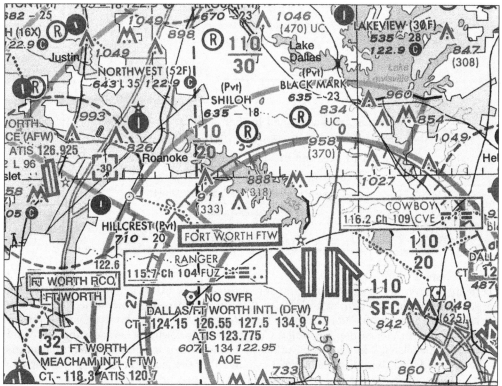

In the late 1940s, the creation of the man-made Grapevine Lake (shown here northwest of the D/FW airport site) displaced many rural residents, some of who moved onto the plains to the south. Ironically, some of those same people were displaced again as the cities of Dallas and Fort Worth purchased land for the new airport. (FFM.)

Contract and Agreement

between

The CITY OF DALLAS, TEXAS

and

The CITY OF FORT WORTH, TEXAS

Dated and Effective as of
April 15, 1968

(Continuing, expanding and further defining the powers and
duties of the Dallas-Fort Worth Regional Airport
Board, creating the Joint Airport Fund of the
Cities and providing for the construction
and operation of the Dallas-Fort Worth
Regional Airport)

One of the steps in creating the Dallas/Fort Worth Regional Airport was the establishment of a permanent governing body to replace the interim six-man board created in 1965. An election was scheduled for June 6, 1967, in both Dallas County and Tarrant County (where Fort Worth was located), to authorize the North Central Texas Regional Airport Authority. Voters in Tarrant County approved the measure, but Dallas County voted it down. At the next interim board meeting four days later, J. Erik Jonsson, still mayor of Dallas, reassured the Fort Worth members of the interim board that his city remained committed to the airport, proposing that the two cities create a joint board of members elected by the two city councils. He further proposed that such a board's membership be based on the two cities' relative populations. Thus it was that an 11-member board was eventually formed, comprising seven representatives from Dallas and four from Fort Worth. These proportions would also apply to all the financing aspects of the airport construction and operations, as outlined in the final agreement, dated April 15, 1968. (D/FW.)

Three

CREATING THE WORLD'S LARGEST AIRPORT

Ground breaking for what would be the world's largest airport took place on Wednesday, December 11, 1968, with a projected opening date of late 1972. The numbers associated with the construction were impressive: runway paving would require three million square yards of concrete, and the control tower would be the world's tallest, at almost 200 feet.

The failure of Dallas County voters to approve a regional airport authority complicated the process of managing the airport. Although the two cities formed a joint board to oversee the airport, that board did not have the power to raise taxes, purchase property, issue revenue bonds, or perform the other functions of the proposed airport authority. Fort Worth and Dallas would have to accomplish those tasks themselves, assuming, respectively, four-elevenths and seven-elevenths of the fiscal responsibility.

To promote the new airport, executive director Thomas Sullivan and the airport board created the North Texas Commission, a select group of civic and business leaders. As part of a $1.5 million inaugural marketing effort, the commission coined the name Southwest Metroplex—later shortened to Metroplex—to describe the greater Dallas–Fort Worth area. The term quickly gained acceptance and remains in use today.

Construction began in January 1969, shortly after the last airline flights departed Greater Southwest International Airport to the south. Delays in awarding a contract for the AirTrans people mover pushed the projected 1972 opening date to July 1973, and other factors combined to postpone the date further, to October. Finally, concern on the part of the airlines that the airport would not be ready for the upcoming 1973 holiday season pushed the date to January 1974.

Notwithstanding the most recent changes to the opening date, there was no need to delay the September 1973 dedication, since the majority of the facilities had been completed. With former governor John Connally as commissioner general of the dedication ceremonies, the airport hosted a four-day, $450,000 Texas-sized gala.

Ground breaking for the new Dallas/Fort Worth Regional Airport took place on December 11, 1968, only nine days after the first $35 million in bonds were issued to cover initial construction costs. Shown at the ceremony are, from left to right, Secretary of Transportation Alan S. Boyd, Dallas mayor and airport board member J. Erik Jonsson, board vice president J. Lee Johnson III, and executive director Thomas Sullivan. (D/FW.)

The first step in making D/FW a reality was moving about 200,000 cubic yards of earth. This was accomplished in the first few months by 100 workers with 27 earth scrapers and 18 bulldozers. To support that effort, a pipeline was built from Fort Worth to bring water to the site, without which this undramatic but very necessary first step could not be accomplished. (D/FW.)

During excavation for the new airport, workers began uncovering fossil remains that were soon identified as those of a 70-million-year-old plesiosaur from the Cretaceous period. The area was a seabed at that time, and the 25-foot-long creature used porpoise-like flippers to move through the water. Braniff International Airways underwrote the cost of restoration, done by Southern Methodist University paleontology professor Bob Slaughter and his graduate students. Here, Braniff flight hostess Pam Kretlow poses with the skeleton, which was displayed in Braniff's Terminal 2W. (UTD.)

Another artifact from the airport site's natural history is this sample of iron pyrite (fool's gold), known as "D/FW pyrite." This type of pyrite growth is found only on the airport site. This sample was discovered by airport board member Jan Collmer in a creek bed that is now covered by runway 17L-35R. (Author.)

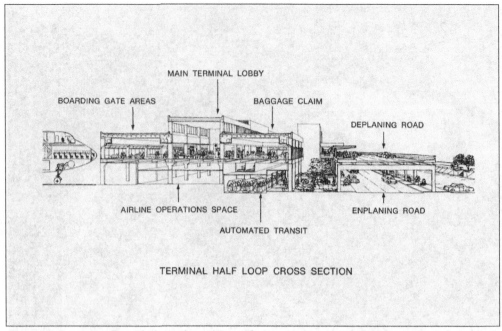

MAIN TERMINAL LOBBY

BOARDING GATE AREAS

BAGGAGE CLAIM

DEPLANING ROAD

AIRLINE OPERATIONS SPACE

ENPLANING ROAD

AUTOMATED TRANSIT

TERMINAL HALF LOOP CROSS SECTION

As construction progressed, the utility of Gyo Obata's semicircular design for a series of passenger terminals became more evident. The cross-sectional diagram (above) shows how arrival and departure traffic are separated in different levels. The lower level accommodates arriving passengers, whether by car or the AirTrans automated people mover. The upper level features boarding areas on the outer perimeter, while the baggage claim areas on the same level open on to the upper-level roadway. Close-in parking is available inside the semicircular structure. The multilevel configuration of the design is apparent in the photograph (below) of Terminal 2W. The building is approximately 80-percent complete. (Both, UTD.)

In 1971, the airport board hired Leonard "Len" Limmer, police chief of the Dallas suburb of Mesquite and the youngest police chief in Texas, as chief of airport security. With executive director Thomas Sullivan's approval, Limmer created a versatile Department of Public Safety (DPS) force that was cross-trained in firefighting, aircraft fire and rescue, and emergency medical services, in addition to law enforcement. His concept met with initial resistance, but would later prove its worth several times over. Limmer's officers went through rigorous training at various academies, including the FBI's Quantico, Virginia, facility. They also trained with foreign security forces to prepare for possible international hijacking situations. By the time the airport opened in January 1974, D/FW's 300 uniquely qualified officers made up one of the most well-trained public safety departments in the world. Above, Limmer (center) confers with Jim Woods, his original fire chief (left), Ray Henson, his police chief (second from left), and Bob Winters, the DPS assistant director (far right). The man with his back to the camera is unidentified. (D/FW.)

Construction for the airport's control tower began in 1972. Rising 196 feet over the nearly completed airport complex, it would be the world's tallest control tower at the time. Inside the 620-square-foot cab, one set of air traffic controllers would oversee traffic on the east side of the airport, while another team would control arrivals and departures on the west side. (D/FW.)

The airport's control tower was completed in time for a dedication ceremony on January 10, 1974. Shown at the ribbon-cutting ceremony are, from left to right, Fort Worth mayor R.M. Stovall, US representative Dale Milford, Dallas mayor Wes Wise, FAA administrator Alexander Butterfield, airport board chair J. Erik Jonsson, William F. McKee, Henry L. Newman, board vice chair J. Lee Johnson III, and US representative Alan Steelman. (D/FW.)

The first official landing of an aircraft at D/FW occurred on May 17, 1973, when a Coast Guard Falcon jet brought Secretary of Transportation Claude S. Brinegar to inspect the facility. At that time, the airport was 88-percent complete. (D/FW.)

As airport construction progressed, commercial traffic at GSIA declined, until the last scheduled airline flight departed in 1968. However, during D/FW's construction, flight activity continued at GSIA in the form of charter operations as well as airline training flights, mostly with American Airlines Boeing 727s (shown here) and an occasional DC-10, and, sometimes, by Delta Air Lines. (William W. Sierra.)

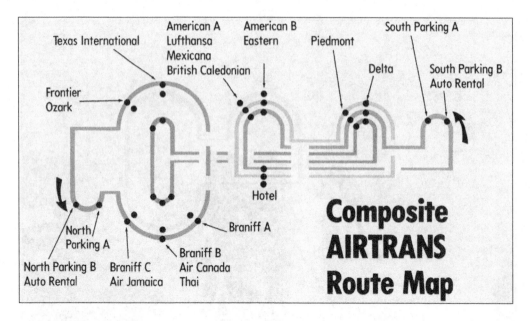

Composite AIRTRANS Route Map

Texas International
American A
Lufthansa
Mexicana
British Caledonian
American B
Eastern
Piedmont
South Parking A
Delta
South Parking B
Auto Rental
Frontier
Ozark
North/
Parking A
North Parking B
Auto Rental
Braniff C
Air Jamaica
Braniff B
Air Canada
Thai
Braniff A
Hotel

To transfer passengers from one terminal to another or to remote parking lots, D/FW's construction committee envisioned an automated people mover instead of the buses used at most airports. Automated cars would run on rubber tires in a U-shaped roadway along a 12-mile route (shown in the map above), and the estimated average waiting time for a car at any point along the route was 10 minutes. Although not the lowest bidder, LTV Aerospace of nearby Grand Prairie was awarded the contract for the AirTrans system due to a belief that its design was better and that, as a local company, it could better service the system (which turned out not to be the case). Below, an AirTrans test car moves out of the partially completed Terminal 2W in December 1972. (Above, FFM; below, D/FW.)

One of the first instances of the name Metroplex to describe the greater Dallas–Fort Worth area is in this advertisement created by the North Texas Commission to market the new D/FW Regional Airport. In addition to comparing the size of the airport to Manhattan Island, the advertisement points out that D/FW is within four hours' nonstop flying time to any mainland US city. (FFM.)

In 1971, the airport board contracted with AMFAC of Honolulu to build a 450-room hotel on the west side of the International Parkway. The Airport Marina Hotel was billed as the only hotel in the area "with its own international airport." The Air Line Pilots Association expressed concern about the hotel's location near the control tower, but the Federal Aviation Administration declared that the hotel's placement was not hazardous. (D/FW.)

An airport as big as Manhattan.

It's the nation's largest airport. And the most efficient for airlines and passengers. The new Dallas/Fort Worth Airport, just 25 minutes from downtown Dallas or Fort Worth. A $500 million facility spread over 17,000 acres. That's three times as big as Kennedy, and larger than Manhattan Island.

This enormous land area (9 miles long, 8 miles wide) solves the major problems facing existing airports. We'll have uncongested airspace. Plenty of room for runways, aprons, terminals, parking and air cargo facilities. At opening there will be four multi-level terminals with a total of 65 passenger gates, all capable of handling the new generation of aircraft. Passenger parking will be within 500 feet of boarding. At

maturity, the airport complex will include 225 passenger gates, fronting an 18-lane linear spine freeway. By 1985, we will handle over 100,000 passengers daily.

Air cargo design and capacity are equally as bold. The ultimate plan provides for two separate air cargo cities. A total of 200 fully automated gates capable of handling as much cargo as any seaport in the world.

We're right in the middle of things.

Our location is equidistant between the 4 major population centers of North America—New York, Chicago, Los Angeles and Mexico City. And the new airport can only add to our importance as an economic center. Already, Dallas and Fort Worth have exceeded national growth rate to become the largest metropolitan region in the Southwest. Today 2.3 million people in an 11-county area, and a projected 4 million by 1985.

True, the sky is our ocean, putting us within 4 hours non-stop to any U.S. mainland city, within 14 hours to any country in the world. But our area is also served by six spokes of Interstate Highway systems, 4 U.S. highways, 7 major State highways and 9 rail lines.

Industrial sites and office space.

The Dallas/Fort Worth area has long been oriented toward a healthy business climate and corporate

profits. Dun & Bradstreet reports that only New York and Chicago have more million dollar companies than Dallas/Fort Worth. The Airport can only accelerate this trend. Today, an unprecedented number of industrial parks dot our 11-county area. Plus, more than 5 million square feet of new office space. Obviously, the local business community has made a hard dollar commitment to growth.

What is The Southwest Metroplex?

Simply stated, The Southwest Metroplex is a complex of metropolitan areas. A planned 11-county economic region encompassing more than 8,360 square miles. It's a megapolis with leg room.

There's a lot more to our story. And if you'd like to learn more, we'll send information on The Southwest Metroplex, industrial sites, office space, quality of life and the new Dallas/Fort Worth Airport.

Write: Mr. Richard D. Jones, Executive Director, North Texas Commission, 600 Avenue H East, Suite 101, Dept. 1409, Arlington, Texas 76011. Telephone 817/265-7101.

Dallas/Fort Worth
The Southwest Metroplex®

51

Former Texas governor and former secretary of the treasury John Connally was selected to serve as commissioner general for the D/FW Regional Airport's four-day dedication ceremony, September 20–23, 1973. The airport board authorized $450,000 for the event, which would include a press day, a 5,000-guest charity gala, a formal dedication, and a public open house. (D/FW.)

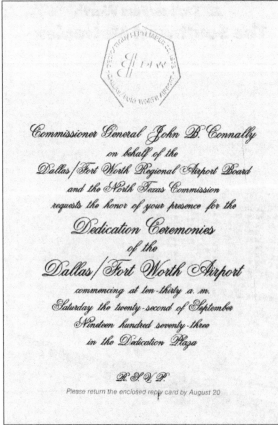

Commissioner General John B. Connally
on behalf of the
Dallas/Fort Worth Regional Airport Board
and the North Texas Commission
requests the honor of your presence for the

Dedication Ceremonies
of the
Dallas/Fort Worth Airport
commencing at ten-thirty a. m.
Saturday the twenty-second of September
Nineteen hundred seventy-three
in the Dedication Plaza

R S V P
Please return the enclosed reply card by August 20

Over 1,500 copies of this invitation were sent to heads of state, ambassadors, and national and international dignitaries for the airport's official dedication on Saturday, September 22, the third day of the four-day event. Other invitations were sent to some 40,000 individuals all over the globe. Officials from over 50 countries attended the dedication activities. (UTD.)

This 160-page program commemorates the dedication ceremony for D/FW, which began on September 20, 1973, with an International Press Day. The four-day celebration concluded with open houses on the last two days, with air shows featuring flight demonstrations of the supersonic Concorde airliner. VIP events featured dignitaries from over 50 nations and entertainers such as Willie Nelson, Peter Nero, and Doc Severinsen. (FFM.)

The official D/FW dedication ceremony in September 1973 featured the first landing of a supersonic British/French Concorde airliner in the United States, as indicated on this souvenir poster given to visitors. The airport was designed with supersonic transports in mind, but it would be over five years before the Concorde operated on a regular schedule from D/FW, and then only for 16 months. (FFM.)

On the opening day of the airport's dedication, September 20, 1973, official visitors and Braniff employees were treated to the rare sight of a supersonic Concorde, parked at Braniff International's Terminal 2W. It sat next to *747 Braniff Place*, the promotional name the company had given its Boeing 747. The Concorde had arrived from Caracas, Venezuela, with a passenger list of Braniff executives, international press representatives, and European dignitaries. (UTD.)

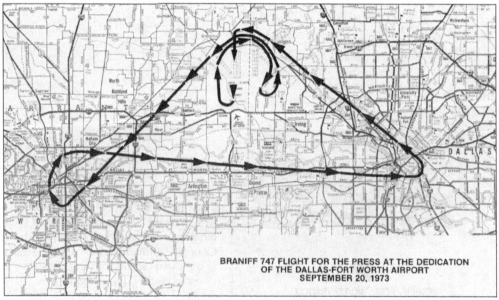

BRANIFF 747 FLIGHT FOR THE PRESS AT THE DEDICATION
OF THE DALLAS-FORT WORTH AIRPORT
SEPTEMBER 20, 1973

Later that day, *747 Braniff Place* took media representatives on a press flight from D/FW around the local area. This map shows the route, beginning with a circuit of the airport proper, followed by a loop around the downtown areas of Fort Worth and then Dallas before returning to what was then the world's largest airport. (UTD.)

Among the dignitaries on hand at the display of *747 Braniff Place* and the Concorde on Thursday, September 20, was Braniff CEO Harding L. Lawrence. He had travelled to Europe to lobby Concorde officials to bring the supersonic airliner to D/FW for the official dedication ceremonies. Under Lawrence's tenure, Braniff would operate Concordes from D/FW to Dulles International Airport, but it would prove to be a bad business decision. (UTD.)

Following Thursday's press day activities, an international-themed charity gala in Terminal 4E was held the following evening for over 5,000 invited guests. The international atmosphere was highlighted by 14 separate party areas, each offering food prepared by European chefs and entertainment from a different part of the world. Decorations included hundreds of potted tropical trees and colorful flowers. (D/FW.)

Celebrity performers at the $50-per-person Friday night charity gala included Peter Nero, Willie Nelson, and Doc Severinsen (shown here) and his band. Unfortunately, over 2,000 unexpected guests also attended, creating traffic jams and parking problems that caused commissioner general Connally and other dignitaries to be late. After the event, some guests waited an hour or more to reclaim their valet-parked vehicles. (D/FW.)

At the formal dedication ceremony on Saturday, September 22, airport board chair J. Erik Jonsson (foreground) spoke of the drama of the ten years leading up to that day, describing the new airport as something that at times had been called the "impossible dream." He also noted that Dallas and Fort Worth had accomplished the dream through a "reshaping of longtime antagonistic attitudes" to create "something of a miracle." (D/FW.)

Over 1,000 national and local dignitaries welcomed an international crowd of 45,000 guests for the airport's official dedication. Ross Newmann, the CAB examiner who had ruled 10 years earlier that Dallas and Fort Worth would have to agree on a common airport, praised the "cooperation, trust, faith, and good will" of the cities, characterizing D/FW as a model airport for years to come. (D/FW.)

The final day of D/FW's four-day dedication celebration, Sunday, September 23, brought thousands of visitors for a public open house featuring the world's largest static aircraft display and a Texas-sized air show. In a special edition of that day's *Dallas Times-Herald*, airport executive director Thomas Sullivan describes the 10-year process of building the airport as "the kind of opportunity that comes once in a lifetime." (D/FW.)

UNITED STATES OF AMERICA
DEPARTMENT OF TRANSPORTATION
FEDERAL AVIATION ADMINISTRATION

AIRPORT OPERATING CERTIFICATE

This certifies that   DALLAS-FORT WORTH REGIONAL AIRPORT
    owned and operated by the DALLAS-FORT WORTH REGIONAL AIRPORT BOARD

has met the requirements of the Federal Aviation Act of 1958, as amended, and the rules, regulations, and standards prescribed thereunder for the issuance of this certificate, and is hereby authorized to operate as a certificated airport in accordance with and subject to said Act and the rules, regulations, and standards prescribed thereunder, including but not limited to 14 CFR Part 139, and any additional terms, conditions, and limitations contained herein, or in the currently approved Airport Operations Manual on file with the Federal Aviation Administration.
This certificate is not transferable and, unless sooner surrendered, suspended or revoked, shall continue in effect

Effective date: July 1, 1973

Issued at   Fort Worth, Texas
       June 29, 1973

By Direction of the Administrator

Director, Southwest Region

One of the final official steps toward D/FW's opening was the approval of the airport's operating certificate by the Federal Aviation Administration (FAA). The certificate bears the signature of FAA southwest regional director Henry Newman, who was instrumental in shepherding the airport project through the federal approval process. (D/FW.)

William G. Fuller, whose aviation career with Fort Worth began in 1925 (see page 12), and who was the city's director of aviation from 1950 to 1961, surveys the Greater Southwest International Airport's empty terminal building in March 1974. The last commercial airline flight from the airport had departed over five years earlier, and all flight operations were now suspended with the opening of D/FW immediately to the north. (UTD.)

Four

THE AIRPORT
OF THE METROPLEX

In the early morning of Sunday, January 13, 1974, Dallas/Fort Worth Regional Airport began commercial aviation operations, and Dallas's Love Field ceased to become the world's 10th-busiest airport. When D/FW opened, it was the biggest airport in the world. It was also the most expensive, with a final price tag of $700 million. It had three runways, four separate terminal buildings, and 56 boarding gates. The airport welcomed nine major airlines and eight commuter carriers, operating flights to 226 destinations, including two in Mexico.

Shortly after the airport's opening, executive director Thomas Sullivan, who had shepherded the airport from its first plans to opening day, resigned for health reasons. Sullivan was succeeded by his deputy, Ernest Dean, who, as resident manager for TAMS, had overseen the airport's original site selection. When Dean was forced to step down in 1985 (see page 85), Vernell Sturns served as interim CEO until Los Angeles airport executive Oris Dunham was hired by the D/FW board. Sturns would later serve a term as executive director in his own right, followed in 1994 by Jeff Fegan, who served until 2013.

In 1978, President Carter signed the Airline Deregulation Act, allowing new air carriers to start operations and establish new routes without a long approval process. These new carriers were able to offer low fares, undercutting established airlines, some of which were carrying large amounts of debt. However, D/FW saw increased international traffic as a result of deregulation.

As the new airport began operations, its leadership continued to pursue one of the original planners' goals of developing D/FW into not only a prominent national aviation center, but a global aviation gateway to the Metroplex for both passengers and cargo. As a result, both domestic and international air carriers were offering nonstop or direct service to almost 40 foreign destinations by the airport's 25th anniversary.

A crowd of over 1,000 people was on hand for the first arrival at the new Dallas/Fort Worth Regional Airport. American Airlines Flight 341 arrived from New York via Memphis and Little Rock, at 12:07 a.m. on January 13, 1974. In the photograph above, the first passengers, Dr. J.W. Parker (center, in checkered coat) and his wife, Patricia, are presented with a silver commemorative medallion. The Parkers are flanked by Dallas mayor Wes Wise (left) and Fort Worth mayor R.M. "Sharkey" Stovall (right). All other passengers received a bronze medallion and a "first flight" certificate. The flight arrived exactly on schedule, piloted by Capt. Vern Peterson. In the photograph below, Peterson (right) is being met by airport manager Fred Ford. (Both, D/FW.)

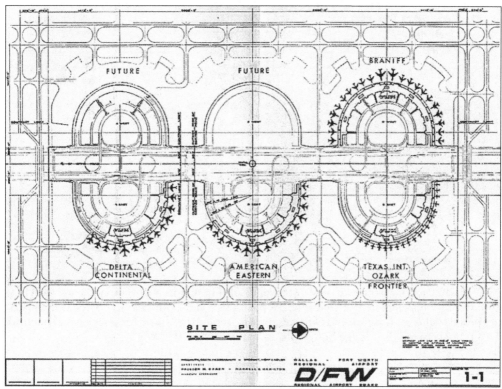

This early airport site plan, with north to the right, shows the projected initial use of the four semicircular terminals. Braniff, the airport's largest tenant, would occupy virtually all of Terminal 2 West (top right). The other airlines would use the terminals east of the International Parkway, designated, from right to left, 2E ("2 East"), 3E, and 4E. (D/FW.)

In this south-facing view, the four semicircular terminals of Dallas/ Fort Worth Regional Airport are shown shortly after the January 1974 opening. Braniff International, the airport's largest tenant, occupied Terminal 2W (for "2 West") at lower right, while eight other airlines and eight commuter carriers shared space at the partially completed terminals across the International Parkway. (D/FW.)

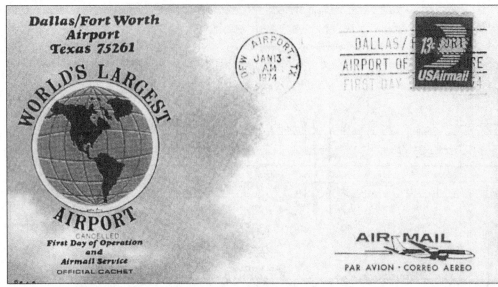

D/FW was so large, it was given its own zip code, 75261. The airport board authorized a special first day cover to commemorate the beginning of operations and of postal service. A 130,000-square-foot postal facility at the south end of the airport also served the North Texas region and handled the airmail between the United States, Mexico, and Canada. (D/FW.)

From the beginning, Mexicana Airlines shared space with Braniff at Terminal 2W. Even though it would be 11 years before "Regional" was replaced with "International" in the airport's name, Mexicana offered daily flights to two Mexican cities, and half the pending route applications of other airlines were for international destinations. (FFM.)

Shortly after D/FW's opening, Metroflight Airlines began offering commuter service with 19-passenger De Havilland Twin Otters from Love Field into the new airport (right). The $10 one-way fare compared favorably to a taxi ride, which could cost up to twice as much, and passengers were assured that their luggage would be transferred to their flight out of D/FW. Metroflight discontinued the service the following September as being uneconomical, but continued flying to D/FW from towns in East Texas. Rio Airways, shown parked next to the large jets at Braniff's Terminal 2W (below), was another commuter airline that provided a similar service from other towns. By 1977, eight commuter airlines operating a variety of smaller aircraft were providing service into D/FW from outlying Texas locations. (Right, *Dallas Morning News*; below, D/FW.)

LOVE FIELD TO DFW AIRPORT IN SEVEN MINUTES.

Introducing MetroFlight Airlines.

The new Dallas-Fort Worth Regional Airport. Beautiful, modern, as big as the island of Manhattan.

And sometimes it seems to be almost as far away.

If you seem to be spending more time on the ground trying to get into the air these days, here's good news.

MetroFlight Airlines will fly 62 times a day between Love Field and DFW Airport. There's a flight every half-hour from 6:00 a.m. to 10:30 p.m. daily. The trip takes seven minutes. That's right, *seven minutes*.

You'll fly in air-conditioned comfort on popular, 19-passenger De Havilland Twin Otters, which utilize special short take-off landing strips close to the terminal. This avoids the main landing strips and possible delays due to airport congestion.

MetroFlight is easy and convenient. Park your car at Love Field, and purchase your round-trip ticket at the Braniff counter.

And here's the good part. You only need one ticket. The ticket you purchase can include both your MetroFlight and any connecting flight to anywhere on any airline. And your baggage will be checked straight through. No hassle between planes.

You're assured a smooth, easy trip, because Metro is no newcomer to the airline business. With more flights in and out of Houston Intercontinental Airport than any other airline, Metro has been serving Houston since 1969.

Easy, convenient, inexpensive, and above all, fast. That's MetroFlight Airlines. Call us for more information. Just dial 638-7690 (just remember Metro 90) or call your travel agent.

Next time you're flying out of DFW, fly out of Love. On MetroFlight Airlines. We put time saving back into air travel.

METROFLIGHT AIRLINES

Call METRO-90 or your travel agent for service beginning April 1.

Metro Airline Designator FY

Braniff
International
System Route Map

In 1976, Braniff, the airport's largest tenant, broke ground for a new corporate complex, to be called Braniff Place. The new facility, opened in December 1978, was much more than the airline's corporate headquarters. With a man-made lake and acres of green space, the facility also featured a training center for the airline's pilots and flight hostesses, a hotel for trainees and crew layovers, and an extensive recreation area for Braniff employees. (UTD.)

At 7:00 p.m. on March 18, 1978, Braniff began the first nonstop service from D/FW to Europe with a flight to London (Gatwick). This promotional flier emphasizes the new service, with a bold red line marking the route against a black-and-white background. (UTD.)

On January 12, 1979, two Concordes (above), with Braniff captains Glenn Shoop and Ken Larson at the controls, landed within one second of each other on parallel runways to inaugurate Braniff's Concorde service between D/FW and Europe. Operating the Concordes through an interchange agreement with British Airways and Air France, Braniff crews flew the aircraft between D/FW and Dulles International Airport in Washington, DC. The European crews flew the transatlantic route to and from London or Paris. The first day cover (below) commemorates the beginning of outbound Concorde service to Europe from D/FW on January 13, 1979. Braniff's Concorde flights suffered from low passenger volume, and the service was discontinued in May 1980. (Above, D/FW; below, Randy Hinshaw Collection.)

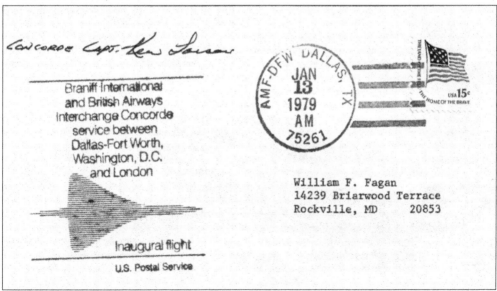

In 1979, American Airlines moved its headquarters to Fort Worth from New York after years of courtship by the Metroplex business community. CEO Al Casey (left) believed the relocation would improve the airline's tenuous cash position, partly through a projected 20-year savings of $200 million in facilities rental alone. Yet to be calculated were savings in productivity due to D/FW's outstanding facilities. American already had an extensive flight-crew training operation in the area, and D/FW was one of the airline's major hubs. The move was well timed; with the demise of Braniff in 1982 (see page 82), American was positioned to take over many of Braniff's routes and become the largest airline at D/FW. That same year, American inaugurated nonstop service from D/FW to two significant destinations in opposite directions, Hawaii and London, with its Boeing 747s, one of which is shown in the photograph below. (Both, D/FW.)

From the very beginning, D/FW was designed to become an international air cargo center, with an air freight facility at either end of the airport. Both domestic and foreign cargo carriers accounted for a steady increase in operations, resulting in the airport doubling its freight handling area in 1981. (D/FW.)

On the occasion of the airport's 25th anniversary in January 1999, the airport opened its International Cargo Centre on the west side, adding another 205,000 square feet to its existing 2.1 million square feet of cargo handling space. That year, the amount of cargo at D/FW would peak at over 920,000 tons. (Author.)

Some of the land purchased for the airport had been farmland, and in at least one case the former owners leased the property back from the airport to continue farming. This not only generated revenue, but freed the airport from the task of maintaining the property. The practice was eventually discontinued, however, as the crops attracted birds, which constituted a flight safety hazard. (D/FW.)

The Airline Deregulation Act of 1978 lessened restrictions on air fares and new routes, enabling new carriers to begin operations unburdened by the debt that many established airlines were carrying from higher fuel costs and lower passenger volumes. By 1982, several new airlines, such as America West, had begun service at D/FW, adding to the airport's total air traffic count. (D/FW.)

In just a few years of operation, D/FW experienced a phenomenal growth in international passenger and cargo traffic. In 1978, over 400,000 international passengers came through the airport's customs facility (above) as direct arrivals from other countries. In 1979, the airport's status was elevated from a port of entry to a Customs District by the US Department of Customs. That same year, the Commerce Department's Travel Service awarded gateway status to the airport, making D/FW eligible for promotion in foreign countries by the US government. Lufthansa Airlines (below) was one of four new international carriers that began serving the airport in 1980; Lufthansa began service to Frankfurt on May 1. Much of the credit for this international activity went to the North Texas Commission, which worked aggressively to bring foreign air carriers to D/FW. (Above, D/FW; below, Christian Jilg.)

The name of the airport was officially changed to Dallas/Fort Worth International Airport on January 1, 1985, to reflect its growing stature as an international gateway. By that time, the airport had become the sixth-busiest in the world, and its domestic and international airlines offered service to over 20 international destinations on three continents. (D/FW.)

On May 15, 1989, the Boeing 747 Shuttle Carrier Aircraft (SCA) was transporting the Shuttle orbiter *Atlantis* back to Florida's Kennedy Space Center following a landing at Edwards Air Force Base, California. The original plan was to land at Barksdale Air Force Base, Louisiana, but weather conditions there caused the plane to land at D/FW instead. This was the first and only time the SCA landed at a commercial airport. (D/FW.)

In 1988, Delta Air Lines opened a satellite terminal southeast of its area in Terminal 4E (now Terminal E) to accommodate its expanding hub operations. Passenger access from the main terminal was through an underground tunnel dubbed "Easy Street" by Delta's marketing department. When Delta closed its hub and significantly reduced its flight operations in 2005, the satellite was closed. (D/FW.)

As part of a 1997 master plan, the airport board voted to change the existing terminal designations. The original numbered "West" and "East" designations were functional for the original planners, but had little meaning to airport users. The new alphabetical designations shown here reflect the order of the exit ramps for each terminal as encountered while driving north to south on the central International Parkway. (D/FW.)

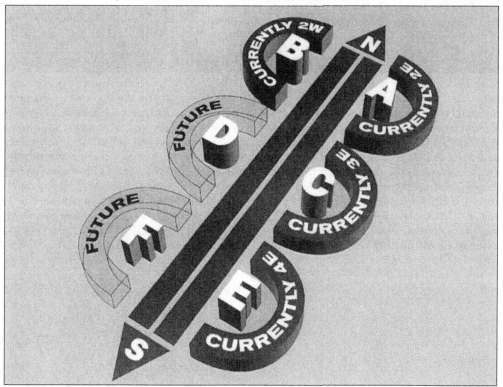

As this north-facing view was taken in late 1998, Dallas/Fort Worth International Airport was preparing to celebrate its 25th anniversary. With seven runways, three control towers, and four terminal buildings, it was the third-busiest airport in the world. With an average of nearly 2,300 flights a day, the airport was serving 60 million passengers annually to and from over 150 cities, including 38 international destinations. By then, D/FW had also proven to be a strong economic catalyst for the Metroplex. The majority of the 16 Fortune 500 companies in the area specifically cited the airport as the reason for their location in North Texas. In the airport's silver anniversary annual report, executive director Jeff Fegan (who had succeeded Vernell Sturns in 1994) reiterated the organization's commitment to the highest level of customer service. He also proudly noted that in 1998, the average operational cost per enplaned passenger at D/FW was just $2.08—a remarkable statistic when compared to the $5 per-passenger figure at Dallas's Love Field 45 years earlier (see page 27). (D/FW.)

Five

CHALLENGES AND SOLUTIONS

As D/FW grew and flight operations multiplied, many difficult situations arose to test the mettle of the organization's board and staff. Comprehensive, well-thought-out solutions to complex problems and rapid, effective reaction to emergencies characterized the airport's responses to these challenges and reflected great credit on all levels of airport leadership.

One of the most vexing situations for the airport's leadership began even before the airport opened. In a 1969 agreement, airlines serving the Metroplex pledged to move to D/FW when it opened and to cease operations from other area airports, including Dallas's Love Field. Southwest Airlines, a new low-cost carrier, began flying out of Love Field in 1971 to other Texas cities and declined to move to D/FW in 1974. Its business model, Southwest stated, was based on operating from Love, and in any case, it was not a signatory to the 1969 agreement. After a complicated series of legal actions, the matter was eventually decided in Southwest's favor, allowing it to continue operating from Love Field—although restrictions would later be placed on its operations.

The Airline Deregulation Act of 1978, which the major airlines strongly opposed, had its most negative effect on the airport through the fate of its largest tenant, Braniff International. The airline had expanded ambitiously when deregulation was established, but the passenger volume to support the expansion did not materialize due to a poor economy, forcing the airline into bankruptcy.

In 1985 and again in 1988, D/FW experienced two major accidents involving Delta Air Lines that resulted in loss of life. In both cases, the wisdom of D/FW's planners in placing the airport inside a large perimeter aided recovery efforts. Because both crashes occurred on airport property, its Department of Public Safety (DPS) was able to arrive quickly at the scene.

However, even D/FW's huge 18,000-acre footprint was not large enough to prevent conflict with some surrounding communities as the airport expanded to accommodate an ever-growing demand for air travel. In some cases, D/FW's success as a catalyst for growth in the area had ironically resulted in economic pressures to rezone land close to the airport boundary or under future flight paths from industrial to residential use. This would later cause resistance to the addition of new runways, even though they had always been part of the airport's master plan.

Southwest Airlines, founded by Herb Kelleher (above, left) and Rollin King (right) as a low-cost carrier operating solely within the state of Texas, began flying from Love Field in 1971. The airline kept costs low by flying only one type of aircraft, the Boeing 737 (below), and serving the local commuter from smaller, close-in airports like Love Field. When Southwest declined to move to D/FW, other airlines signaled their intent to continue offering flights out of Love in order to stay competitive. The D/FW board, concerned about a precedent that would weaken its airline revenue base, filed suit in federal court in 1972 to force Southwest to move. A complicated series of legal actions followed, eventually involving the cities of Dallas and Fort Worth as well as several airlines. (Both, Southwest Airlines.)

The legal actions surrounding Southwest Airlines' bid to continue operating out of Love Field went as far as the Supreme Court. When that body refused to hear the case, it let stand a lower court decision in Southwest's favor. Over the next few years, the airline added other Texas cities to its schedule. However, when Southwest announced its intent to begin out-of-state service to New Orleans in 1979, House Majority Leader Jim Wright of Fort Worth (shown here) opposed the move. Another series of legal actions ensued, ending with the CAB's eventual approval for Southwest to serve New Orleans. Wright countered by attaching to a broader piece of transportation legislation an amendment that limited Southwest's (or any other airline's) operations from Love Field. The main provisions of the so-called Wright Amendment were that airlines could not fly nonstop from Love to destinations beyond the four states that bordered Texas, and tickets could not be offered for "one-stop" flights beyond those four states. (Texas Christian University Special Collections.)

One of the few problems on the airport's opening day involved the troubled AirTrans people mover (above), which experienced difficulties during construction and was not yet fully functional. Only that part of the system that operated from terminal to terminal was put in service, while the remote parking lots were served by buses. Even after full service began, the system continued to experience delays and outages, and the entire system had to be shut down in September 1975. The following January, the airport board negotiated a contract settlement with LTV Aerospace, the system's builder, and assumed control of the system. By 1980, AirTrans was operating with high reliability, carrying over seven million passengers annually. On June 24, 1988, car No. 31 (below) became the first car to log one million miles. (Both, D/FW.)

A sluggish economy and high fuel prices combined to make 1980 a difficult time for the airline industry. D/FW experienced a 4-percent drop in passenger traffic, its first decline since opening. The drop occurred despite the addition of three domestic airlines and four international carriers, including Thai International Airways (shown here). Thai International's service to Bangkok through Tokyo made D/FW the only inland airport providing same-plane service to Japan. (D/FW.)

One result of the increase in fuel prices was Braniff's decision to terminate its Concorde service from D/FW to Europe through Dulles International Airport. Concordes were already operating with low passenger loads, and making up for fuel costs through higher ticket prices would discourage potential travelers. The service was discontinued in May 1980, and the proposed Braniff paint scheme (shown here) was never applied to a Concorde. (FFM.)

In 1981, the Professional Air Traffic Controllers Organization (PATCO) threatened to strike over a failure to reach wage and benefit contract terms with the FAA. Although warned that a strike would be illegal since they were federal employees, the controllers began their walkout on Monday, August 3, at 7:00 a.m. The FAA quickly implemented a contingency plan at major airports that included using military air traffic controllers and supervisory personnel (such as at D/FW, seen here) to fill in for the absent controllers. Over one-half of D/FW's flights were cancelled that day, and striking controllers were told to return to work or face termination, fines, and possible imprisonment. By the second day, the situation had improved as some controllers returned, but the airlines still had to reduce their schedules and lost millions of dollars a day. Over 11,000 controllers were fired, and PATCO was dissolved. It would be almost two years before the flight schedules at D/FW were back to their prestrike levels. (D/FW.)

Mitigating the difficulties that challenged the airport in the early 1980s were some positive developments. The East Tower of the Marina Hotel (above) opened in early 1981, adding over 850 rooms to the West Tower's 600. The building names were changed to Amfac Hotel, East Tower and West Tower, and their combined 1,450-plus rooms made the complex the largest hotel complex on any airport property in the world. The hotel system also included the Bear Creek Golf and Racquet Center, with tennis courts, racquetball facilities, and an 18-hole golf course (below) on the southwest corner of the airport property. Another 18 holes were added in 1981. (Both, D/FW.)

On Thursday, May 13, 1982, Braniff International filed for bankruptcy, creating the scene shown here as flight operations ceased once each of the airline's colorful aircraft arrived at Terminal 2W. This was the first major airline bankruptcy in history. Braniff had no cash reserves to continue operating through reorganization proceedings, as has been done in recent years. Believing that the airline industry would be reregulated once Congress and the public became disenchanted with deregulation, Braniff CEO Harding Lawrence had borrowed heavily to acquire aircraft and crews to support a vastly expanded route structure. He envisioned prevailing over his competitors once deregulation was repealed. The repeal did not occur, Lawrence was fired by Braniff's board of directors, and a new executive team was unable to overcome the significant losses due to a perfect storm of high fuel prices, high interest rates, and a bad economy. The impact on D/FW was significant; Braniff was the airport's largest airline and, overnight, ceased paying $21.6 million in annual facility rental and $600,000 in monthly landing fees. (D/FW)

Capt. Gordon Winfield (right) was Braniff International's last captain in the air. He and his crew departed D/FW on May 11, 1982, on Flight 501, one of Braniff's most popular routes—a nonstop to Honolulu. As they approached the West Coast, Winfield and the crew began receiving indications that their airline was ceasing operations and that some aircraft were being ordered to return to D/FW. As he was not specifically ordered to return, Winfield elected to continue. The return flight, number 502, began just before sunset Honolulu time the next day, May 12, as shown in Winfield's last logbook entry (below). After landing at D/FW in the early morning darkness of May 13, Braniff Flight 502 was guided to an empty gate by a lone employee with a flashlight. (Both, Melba Winfield.)

THIS PAGE BEGINS ON			AND ENDS ON			NAME OF AIRLINE				
DATE 19 82	FLIGHT NUMBER	FROM	TO	AIRCRAFT MAKE AND MODEL	AIRCRAFT CERTIFICATE MARK	MILES FLOWN ENGINES	DURATION OF FLIGHT		DAY	NIGHT
5-2	501	DFW	HNL	B-7617-100	N-601BN	JT9-7A		7 35	6 30	1 05
5-7	502	HNL	DFW	"	"	"		7 00		7 00
5-5	501	DFW	HNL	"	"	"		7 48	2 15	5 33
5-6	502	HNL	DFW	"	"	"		6 57		6 57
5-11	501	DFW	HNL	B-7617-100	N-601BN	JT9-7A		7 53	6 22	1 31
5-12	502	HNL	DFW	"	"	"		6 55	05	6 50

IF YOU WISH TO CERTIFY EACH PAGE USE THIS SPACE		
CERTIFIED CORRECT_____	TOTALS FOR THIS PAGE ONLY	44 8	15 12	28 56
ATTESTED BY_____	TOTALS FORWARD FROM PRECEDING PAGE	28 625 57	16 470 19	12 155 38
	GRAND TOTALS FORWARD TO NEXT PAGE	28 670 05	16 485 31	12 184 34

In 1984, Braniff was brought out of bankruptcy by Hyatt Hotel chain founder Jay Pritzker. It flew its first flight as Braniff Inc. from D/FW on March 1. The airline used the paint scheme as shown on this Boeing 727, flying over the Hyatt Regency and Reunion Tower in downtown Dallas. However, the airline was unable to succeed in the highly competitive deregulated environment, and it filed for bankruptcy again in 1989, liquidating all assets. (FFM.)

American Airlines, which had recently moved its corporate headquarters to the Metroplex (see page 66), increased its hub operations at the airport in the wake of Braniff's 1982 bankruptcy. In 1983, American moved into its new corporate buildings just south of the airport. The same year, it began service out of D/FW with its Boeing 767s, as shown here. (American Airlines.)

In 1985, legal action by American Airlines and D/FW against a contractor over the quality of workmanship on American's facilities at Terminal 2E (above) resulted in a subsequent investigation that actually turned against the airport leadership. Irregularities in contract administration as well as examples of mismanagement and misconduct in several areas were uncovered. Some of the practices were in violation of state laws. As a result of the investigation, executive director Ernest Dean and seven other airport executives were forced to step down. The airport board tapped Fort Worth assistant city manager Vernell Sturns (right) to serve as interim executive director. He quickly implemented new contract procedures in addition to policies that strengthened accountability and restored employee morale. Instrumental in repairing the airport's credibility, Sturns would later serve his own term as executive director, succeeding Oris Dunham in 1991. (Above, FFM; right, D/FW.)

As commercial air traffic at D/FW increased again after a downturn in 1980, the airport began construction of runway 13R-31L on its west side (shown here) as part of the original master plan. In response, the community of Southlake to the northwest, citing health, safety, and noise concerns, initiated legal action to limit the runway's use. With the court action pending, the runway began operations in December 1986. (D/FW.)

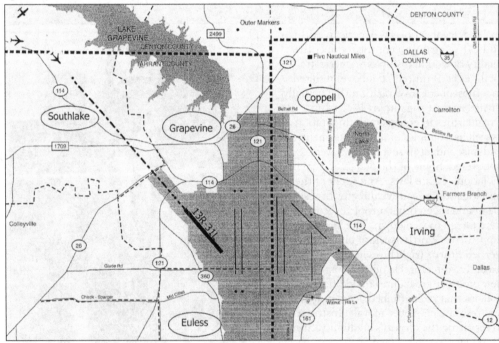

This detail from the D/FW Runway Use Plan shows the relationship of runway 13R-31L to Southlake and the standard arrival route for incoming traffic. The conflict over the new runway was eventually settled, with the airport agreeing to ensure that noise levels remained within established parameters, and Southlake agreeing to curb future residential development within the runway's approach path. (D/FW.)

As D/FW expanded its operations, the leadership worked hard to resolve conflicts with the surrounding communities. In addition to pointing out that expansion efforts were part of the original master plan, officials also cited the airport's role as a major economic catalyst, pointing out examples such as the Las Colinas complex to the east with its 12,000 acres of offices, hotels, and residential areas. (Author.)

Another example of growth in the area around D/FW is the city of Southlake itself, with its vibrant Town Square built in the late 1990s. The city has grown from a population of 5,000 in 1987 to over 26,000 in 2010, with many of its residents attracted by Southlake's proximity to the airport. (Author.)

On August 2, 1985, as thunderstorms dotted the area, Delta Air Lines Flight 191 was on approach to runway 17L when it encountered a microburst—a rare but deadly phenomenon that was just beginning to be understood. This intense downdraft, often produced by a thunderstorm (as depicted in the generic NASA rendering above), can cause an airplane to rapidly lose altitude and airspeed. The Lockheed L-1011 hit the ground once, bounced back into the air, and then hit again on Highway 114 before coming to a rest near the air cargo complex (pictured below) on the airport's northeast corner. Runway 13L is in the background; runway 17L is off the frame to the right. Response from the D/FW DPS was rapid; although 136 passengers and crew perished, the rescue crews were able to save 31 from the burning wreckage. (Above, NASA; below, D/FW.)

On August 31, 1988, another Delta Air Lines disaster occurred at D/FW as Flight 1141, improperly configured for takeoff, crashed shortly after lifting off from runway 18L. The Boeing 727 slid to a fiery stop just north of a perimeter road, still on airport property. Officer Larry Lee Wood was first at the crash site, in his blue-and-white patrol car. Hearing that the flight crew was still trapped inside the cockpit, he retrieved his fire rescue gear from the trunk and entered the aircraft. Fighting heat exhaustion and smoke, he was able to rescue the flight engineer and copilot, enabling other responders to rescue the injured captain. The International Association of Fire Chiefs awarded Wood its prestigious Benjamin Franklin Award for his part in the rescue, and several other DPS members responding to the crash were honored for their extraordinary heroism, which resulted in only 14 of the 108 aboard failing to survive. (D/FW.)

Inspired by his previous experience in the newspaper business, D/FW's director of public affairs, Joe M. Dealey Jr., worked with DPS director Len Limmer and local media to allow direct but supervised access to scenes such as the Delta crashes as long as rescue operations or investigations were not interfered with. This policy was lauded in press industry publications, and it fostered a positive relationship with the media, gaining their cooperation in minimizing disruptions and unauthorized activities. (Joe M. Dealey Jr.)

On January 4, 1987, a Syrian national attempted to hijack an aircraft at the Delta Air Lines terminal (4E) by abducting a 10-year-old boy at gunpoint and demanding to be flown to Egypt. After nine hours of negotiations, D/FW's Sgt. Gary Pinkston convinced the suspect to release the boy and lay down his weapon. This was one of three hijacking attempts at D/FW, none of which was successful. (D/FW.)

90

Six

ON THE MOVE

A modern, well-operated commercial airport is one of the most dynamic places in the world, both in the air and on the ground. Not only airplanes, but private automobiles, rental cars, service vehicles, people, baggage, and even trash need to move efficiently to, from, and throughout the complex. Problems in any one transportation conduit will have an effect on the others. For example, over one-half of D/FW's passengers are connecting to another flight, making it vital for them to quickly proceed to their next gates—whether in the same terminal or not.

From sophisticated electronic navigation equipment for arriving and departing aircraft to the human element of volunteers to assist arriving and departing passengers, all of D/FW's elements are designed to maximize efficiency of movement: the International Parkway, which runs like an arrow for over four miles straight through the airport, keeps vehicle traffic flowing efficiently while allowing easy ramp access to airline terminals; the state-of-the-art automated people mover, Skylink, whisks passengers between its two farthest stations in only nine minutes; and sophisticated electronic navigational equipment allows the airport to accommodate roughly 650,000 aircraft operations (takeoffs and landings) per year.

Not as glamorous as other aspects of an airport, but still important, are the many environmental considerations. From the beginning, the AirTrans system was used to transport D/FW's trash during off-peak operating hours. More recently, the airport has implemented many programs to promote cleaner transportation. A fleet of clean-energy service vehicles prevents hundreds of tons of nitrous oxide emissions from entering the atmosphere, while centralized busing operations reduce the number of vehicles in the airport. Improvements at parking areas, such as Terminal D's smart technology parking system, reduce delays and vehicle idling by indicating the location of available spaces. In addition, D/FW partners with the airlines and the FAA to deploy zero-emission ground service equipment.

Through the benefit of smart design, continuous attention to detail, and well-planned improvements and upgrades, all of the airport's transportation conduits operate in concert to enable a continuous flow of aircraft, vehicles, and people. D/FW is one of the world's most efficient aviation gateways.

One of D/FW's unique features is its six-lane central thoroughfare, the International Parkway, running the north-south length of the airport and allowing for two main airport entrances instead of a conventional single access point that can more easily become congested. After the airport's 1968 ground breaking, Transportation Secretary Alan S. Boyd (see page 46) praised the designers for this feature that, he said, would, in earlier conventional airport planning, have qualified them for "residence in an asylum." In the photograph above, taken shortly before the airport began operations, graceful exit loops facilitate access to the terminals on each side of the thoroughfare. In the 1990s, American Airlines erected large digital signs on the International Parkway listing its departures and arrivals (below). The signs, however, proved to be distracting to drivers and were removed after several accidents were attributed to them. (Both, D/FW.)

D/FW opened in January 1974 with two primary north-south runways, one on each side of the International Parkway, and a single diagonal runway, 13L-31R, on the east side, as seen in this photograph. In 1984, in accordance with the master plan, two additional runways were added, each parallel to and outside of the original two north-south runways. A parallel diagonal runway on the west side, 13R-31L, would follow in 1986. (D/FW.)

Also in 1986, American Airlines, now the airport's largest carrier, opened its own control tower (seen here) to supervise aircraft moving in and out of the boarding gates. The tower also coordinates ground service functions for its airplanes, such as food and beverage service and cabin cleaning. Once away from the terminal area, the planes' movements are directed by FAA controllers. (D/FW.)

As air traffic at D/FW continued to grow, a seventh runway, also in the original master plan, was added to relieve the increasing traffic delays caused by congestion. As a preview to the opening of runway 17L-35R on the east side of the airport, a "Run the Runway" race was held to benefit United Way Charities. Against the backdrop of Delta Air Lines' Boeing 767 *Spirit of Delta*, featuring a special paint scheme for the 1996 Olympic Games in Atlanta, the run took place on September 28, 1996, two days before the runway began operations. However, the celebration was not universal, especially in nearby Grapevine, Irving, Euless, and Coppell. When the runway was initially proposed, those cities had opposed it with legal actions and local ordinances, citing concerns about quality of life and property values. While the eventual resolution with the FAA and in the courts was in D/FW's favor, the airport still provided mitigation far in excess of that required by the runway's environmental impact statement, including purchasing entire residential neighborhoods and soundproofing buildings. (Both, UTD.)

D/FW Airport board member Jan Collmer, in his Extra 300L aerobatic aircraft (above), is one or two seconds away from cutting a ribbon held aloft by two airport employees to open the airport's seventh runway, 17L-35R, on October 1, 1996. Shortly afterward, the first commercial airliner to land on the new runway was American Airlines Flight 486 from Las Vegas. Below, the airport's fire department renders the traditional water cannon salute as Capt. Prudence Kelley guides her Boeing 757 on to the adjoining taxiway. At that time, the airport was serving over 58 million passengers annually with almost 850,000 flights a year. (Both, UTD.)

One of the provisions of the final environmental impact statement for runway 17L-35R requires D/FW to monitor aircraft noise and movements within its airspace to ensure that FAA-approved noise levels are not exceeded. The airport is also required to protect the federal government's investment by doing everything reasonable to prevent incompatible land use encroachment by the surrounding communities. To accomplish this task, the airport's Noise Compatibility Office (NCO), established in 1998, monitors the agendas of local planning and zoning commissions and city councils to determine if incompatible development (such as schools or residences) is being considered within the airport's noise contour. If so, the NCO informs the municipality of the potential conflict and works with it to resolve the issues. The cities surrounding D/FW have agreed to zone compatibility within the airport's noise contour. As a result, the airport has few noise complaints and the residents of the cities have a better quality of life. (Both, D/FW.)

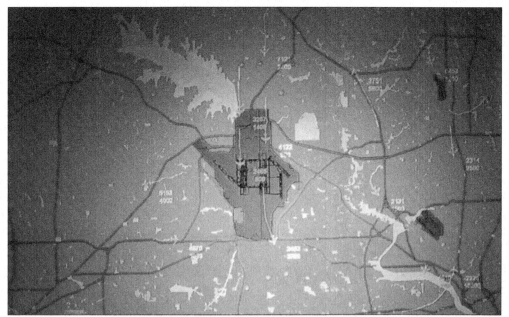

D/FW's NCO has the capability to monitor all individual aircraft movements within the Metroplex. In the image of a large display shown above, aircraft flight tracks can be displayed in real time or recalled with data back to January 1998. D/FW is at the center, and the large body of water to the northeast is Grapevine Lake. Additionally, D/FW's noise monitor array, which covers approximately 110 square miles around the airport with 30 remote monitors, provides and stores both aural and digital noise data. This allows the NCO to ensure compliance with FAA-approved noise contours and to provide accurate responses to complaints and inquiries regarding local air traffic. The display below, covering the same geographic area as the one above, shows the flight patterns for one day's air traffic in and out of the airport. (Both, author.)

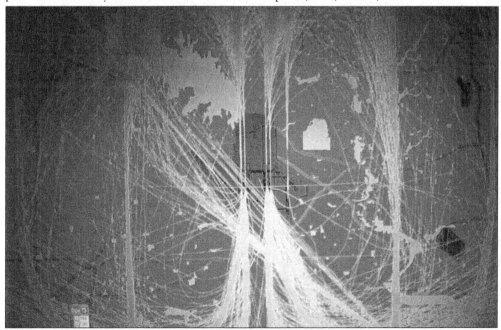

On July 15, 1994, D/FW celebrated the dedication of two new air traffic control towers; one on the east side of the airport, and another (above) on the west. The new towers were built to increase capacity at the airport, which was at the time experiencing up to 2,300 takeoffs and landings daily. The towers allow D/FW to effectively function during peak hours as two separate airports, with each tower controlling air and ground traffic on its side. The original central tower (below) supervises flight clearances and serves as the airport's single control tower for reduced flight operations during nighttime hours. (Above, author; below, D/FW.)

Helping passengers to move through the terminal buildings and throughout the airport, D/FW's volunteer Airport Ambassadors meet arriving and departing travelers and direct them to connecting flights, baggage claim, and other airport facilities. They also provide accurate, up-to-date information about area attractions, hotels, and other amenities. Bilingual Ambassadors provide much-needed services that are greatly appreciated by international visitors. (D/FW.)

The 100-foot tall navigation aid shown here was added to D/FW's air traffic control equipment in 1997. Dubbed "Maverick," its 200-foot-diameter circular antenna sends and receives distance and directional information to and from aircraft within a 150-mile radius. Maverick supplements two similar, but smaller navigational aids, "Cowboy" and "Ranger," to the east and west of the airport, respectively, but not on airport property. (D/FW.)

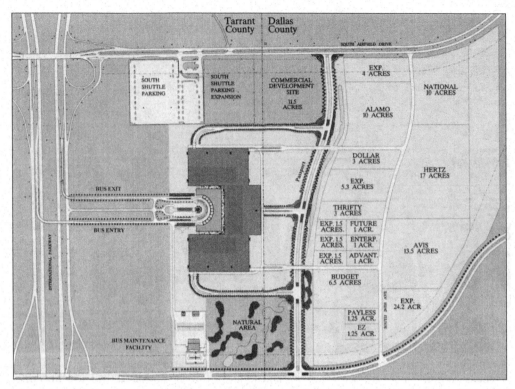

Tarrant
County

Dallas
County

SOUTH AIRFIELD DRIVE

SOUTH
SHUTTLE
PARKING

SOUTH
SHUTTLE
PARKING
EXPANSION

COMMERCIAL
DEVELOPMENT
SITE
11.5
ACRES

EXP.
4 ACRES

NATIONAL
10 ACRES

ALAMO
10 ACRES

DOLLAR
3 ACRES

HERTZ
17 ACRES

BUS EXIT

EXP.
5.3 ACRES

BUS ENTRY

THRIFTY
3 ACRES

INTERNATIONAL PARKWAY

EXP. 1.5
ACRES.

FUTURE
1 ACR.

EXP. 1.5
ACRES.

ENTERP.
1 ACR.

AVIS
13.5 ACRES

EXP. 1.5
ACRES.

ADVANT.
1 ACR.

BUDGET
6.5 ACRES

EXP.
24.2 ACR

NATURAL
AREA

PAYLESS
1.25 ACR.

BUS MAINTENANCE
FACILITY

EZ
1.25 ACR.

In 1998, the airport began work on a $150 million consolidated Rental Car Center on the south side of the airport. The previous 25 years had seen significant growth in car rental activity, and expansion of the existing facilities at each end of the airport was not feasible. Instead of separate buildings for each rental car company, a single terminal building was designed (above), from which all car companies could operate. The terminal's semicircular shape mimics that of the airline terminals (below). This innovative concept in customer service resulted in inquiries from other large airports, most notably Atlanta's Hartsfield International, the nation's busiest airport. (Above, D/FW; below, author.)

Another innovative feature of D/FW's Rental Car Center is the use of a single bus system instead of shuttles operated by each car rental company. A fleet of buses owned by the airport and maintained by the car companies takes passengers between the airport's five airline terminals and the rental center. The buses run every five minutes. (Author.)

Inside the spacious terminal, the traditional crowded line of counters is replaced by large individual spaces for each rental car company, similar to the aircraft boarding gates in an airline terminal. Continuing that similarity, several exits open into a parking garage from which customers retrieve their cars. The lobby also boasts a visitor center where customers can make reservations for hotels, restaurants, and local attractions. (Author.)

The photograph above, with a view looking north and taken in late 2002, shows American Airlines aircraft grouped around Terminal C on the east side of the airport. Visible at the terminal's lower right is a partially completed station for the elevated Skylink people mover, which, within three years, would replace the AirTrans system in use since the airport opened in early 1974. Below, the new Skylink cruises on its track above three AirTrans cars. Skylink began operations on May 21, 2005, with 64 cars moving at speeds of up to 35 miles per hour in both directions. In contrast, the AirTrans system moved in only one direction at a top speed of 17 miles per hour. The decrease in travel time between terminals was especially important for connecting passengers. (Both, D/FW.)

In 2006, D/FW began construction of a new taxiway system designed to significantly reduce daily runway crossings, such as the situation shown at right. An arriving US Airways Boeing 737, inbound to the terminal, is required to wait to cross runway 18L-36R while a Delta Air Lines MD-80 lands. Perimeter taxiways, built out beyond the ends of the runway system, as indicated by the dotted lines in the photograph below, reduce the risk of runway accidents by allowing taxiing aircraft to go around runways instead of crossing them. Efficiency is improved as well; despite the greater distance traveled, arriving aircraft can reach their gates more quickly by not having to hold short of an active runway for landing or departing aircraft. The first section, on the southeast (lower right) side of the airport, was completed in 2008. (Both, D/FW.)

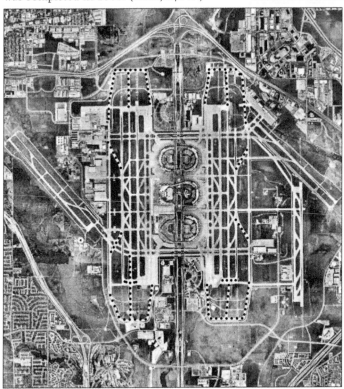

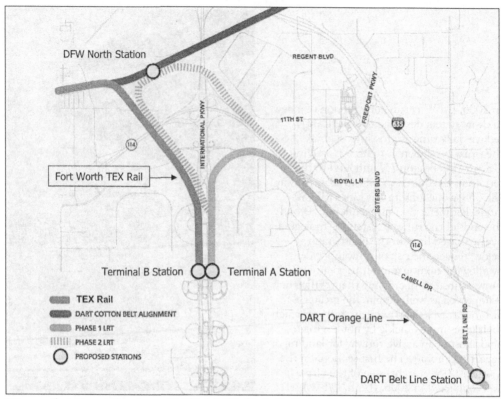

Direct rail service to the airport is scheduled to begin in December 2014 as the Dallas Area Rapid Transit's Orange Line will operate into a rail station at Terminal A, as shown in the rendering above. Service from Fort Worth (the TEX Rail) is planned to begin operation into a station at Terminal B in 2017. The new stations, depicted below, are part of the airport's Terminal Renewal and Improvement Program (see page 124). (Both, D/FW.)

Seven

INTO THE 21ST CENTURY

From the very beginning, the Dallas/Fort Worth International Airport was blessed with farsighted leadership, and the challenge of taking the airport into the 21st century was addressed long before the new millennium dawned. Identifying the airport's most critical needs, airport executives planned a major Capital Development Project (CDP) to be completed by 2005.

Those plans were thrown into disarray by the terrorist attacks of September 11, 2001. The CDP had already been in progress for over a year, and D/FW executives were faced with deciding whether or not to continue the project in the uncertain immediate future of the commercial aviation industry. They boldly decided to forge ahead, and the subsequent success of the project validated their courageous decision.

Three years later, Delta Air Lines announced the elimination of its hub at D/FW, resulting in the eventual withdrawal of 90 percent of its operations at the airport. Even though American Airlines, recovering from its own financial distress, was able to assume some of the vacated routes, the loss of approximately $35 million in landing fees and other related revenue threatened to stifle the airport's slow but steady recovery from the effects of 9/11.

D/FW offered generous financial incentives to any airline that would take over Delta's 24 vacated gates, particularly engaging Southwest Airlines in discussions about the possibility. However, Southwest had another idea to fill the void in North Texas commercial air service left by Delta's reduction in operations. In November 2004, Southwest CEO Gary Kelly announced the beginning of a campaign to repeal the Wright Amendment (see pages 75–77), ending the airline's previously neutral stand on the issue.

The move was immediately opposed by D/FW, American Airlines, the City of Fort Worth, and some members of Congress. As both sides expressed their arguments through media events and grassroots campaigns, a quiet but firm admonition from Sen. Kay Bailey Hutchison (R-Texas) suggested that a locally crafted solution to the situation would best protect the interests of all involved, subtly warning that a congressionally dictated resolution might be harsh and unpopular.

Thus motivated, the parties began negotiations on a Wright Amendment compromise that took many months. An agreement was finally reached in June 2006, the key element of which was that the Wright Amendment restrictions would be lifted by October 2014.

The September 11, 2001, terrorist attacks on the United States sent a shock wave throughout the country, and the nation's air traffic system ground to a halt. By mid-morning, the FAA had stopped takeoffs of all civilian aircraft and ordered all civilian aircraft airborne to land as soon as possible at the nearest airport. By that time, D/FW had logged 211 departures, and by midday, the last of 128 arrivals (scheduled or not) were on the ground. Over 150 aircraft were at terminal gates or parked on taxiways, as seen here. Before flight operations could resume, the FAA required all commercial airports to be recertified with respect to security procedures. D/FW was the first airport in the country to be recertified, and commercial flights resumed on Thursday, September 13, with 377 total arrivals and departures, compared to a normal average of over 2,300. By Saturday, arrivals and departures were at 60 percent of normal, but passenger traffic would not approach pre-9/11 levels for four years. (D/FW.)

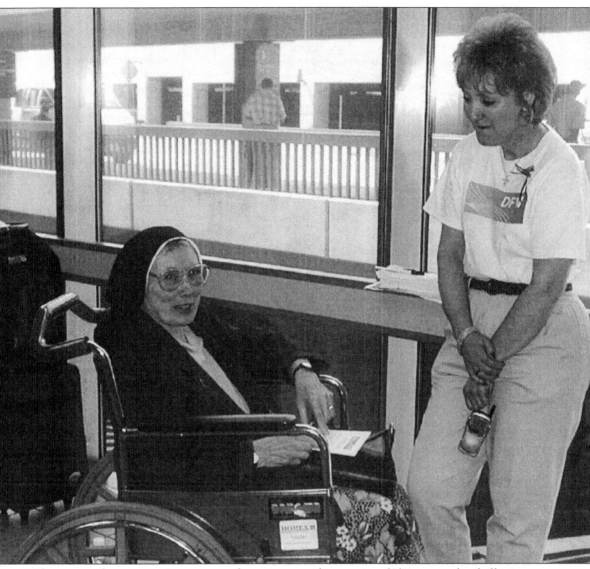

The airport administration's response to the situation on the morning of 9/11 was rapid and effective. As travelers arrived, whether returning from a trip or attempting to depart, D/FW employees were on hand in every terminal. Dressed in white D/FW Airport T-shirts, they assisted passengers with travel needs such as locating their cars, helping with luggage, or giving directions. D/FW was the first major airport to forego parking fees for stranded or displaced passengers, waiving over $300,000 in fees by Saturday, September 15. Officers from the airport's Department of Public Safety, later augmented by 85 federal officers, closed all areas in the terminal past the security checkpoint as each terminal was cleared of passengers and other personnel. Explosive ordnance detection K-9 units were also deployed to all terminals. (D/FW.)

One of the most difficult decisions the airport board had to make after 9/11 was whether or not to continue with a planned $2.7 billion Capital Development Project (CDP), which included expansion of two north-south runways, improvements to the Central Utility Plant, a people mover to replace the AirTrans system, and a new terminal (shown here in an architectural rendering) to service the airport's growing international traffic. (D/FW.)

The decision to continue with the CDP has been characterized as one of the most difficult that the airport leadership has ever had to make, due to reservations about the airline industry's ability to rebound following 9/11. Complicating the financial picture for D/FW was the already-strained financial situation of its largest tenant, American Airlines. Having just completed the acquisition of bankrupt TWA, the airline—along with all other carriers—faced greatly reduced passenger

Once the decision was made to continue with the CDP, it fell to airport board chairman Max Wells (shown here), working with D/FW's chief operating officer, Kevin Cox, to work out a financial strategy to complete funding for the project in a still-uncertain bond market in April 2003. The bond sale netted almost $1.5 billion, the largest of any airport bond sale in US history. (D/FW.)

loads and decreased revenue. With the view that the CDP was designed to take the airport 30 years and more into the future, well beyond the immediate problems related to 9/11, the board decided to continue the project. Construction on the new Terminal D, which had begun in September 2000, continued with an additional $45 million worth of security features and was completed on budget and on time. (D/FW.)

An American Eagle commuter jet takes to the sky as the Dallas/Fort Worth International Airport's Terminal D nears completion for its July 2005 opening. The international terminal, featuring an integrated 12-story Grand Hyatt Hotel, is the signature element of the airport's five-year, $2.7 billion CDP, completed in 2005. With 28 gates and 99 ticketing positions, the facility is capable of supporting 13 million passengers per year. (D/FW.)

Rising dramatically from the middle of Terminal D, the Grand Hyatt Hotel is one of only three hotels worldwide to be integrated into an airport terminal. Through a program authorized by the Transportation Security Administration, hotel guests who are not flying can access the terminal's shops and restaurants, subject to screening and an identity check. The Detroit Metropolitan Wayne County Airport is the only other US airport participating in this program. (D/FW.)

One of the elements of the CDP is a $6 million public art project, featuring paintings, floor mosaics, large-format photography, and sculpture from over 30 local, national, and international artists. Representing D/FW's status as a major international gateway to the United States, the project features art in Terminal D as well as at the Skylink terminal stations. In front of Terminal D, under the arrival canopy, are four sculptures on loan from Dallas's world-famous Nasher Sculpture Center. In the photograph above, Nasher Sculpture Center founder Raymond Nasher (left) confers with D/FW's CEO Jeff Fegan (center) and COO Kevin Cox. At right, American artist Mac Whitney's *Chicota* is installed as one of four sculptures in the D/FW Sculpture Garden at Terminal D. (Both, D/FW.)

On June 25, 2005, D/FW hosted "Texas Day" to showcase the new Terminal D to the North Texas public. The daylong party featured a diverse group of international entertainers, walking tours of the two-million-square-foot terminal, and a chance the meet the artists whose works were featured as permanent installations at the facility. (D/FW.)

On July 23, the first day of flight operations for Terminal D, Capt. Isaias Cruz of D/FW's DPS Fire Honor Guard salutes Mexicana Flight 178, an Airbus 319 from Zacatecas. This was the first flight to arrive at the new terminal. Later in the day, a Korean Air Boeing 747 from Seoul was the first arrival from the Asian continent. (D/FW.)

Southwest Airlines' announced campaign to repeal the Wright Amendment met with quick opposition from D/FW, American Airlines, the City of Fort Worth, and members of Congress, including Rep. Joe Barton (R-Ennis/Arlington). Here, Barton holds a town hall meeting in Terminal D. For its part, D/FW was once again concerned about losing more of its airline revenue base as it prepared for a projected loss of $35 million annually due to Delta's drastic reduction in service. (D/FW.)

In discussions between the major parties in the Wright Amendment debate, Dallas mayor Laura Miller (left) and Fort Worth mayor Mike Moncrief, members of the D/FW board, guided the often intense negotiations to an amenable compromise. Their mutual friendship and respect were a far cry from the earlier Dallas–Fort Worth airport conflicts, when the cities' mayors hardly spoke to each other. (D/FW.)

On June 15, 2006, the principal parties involved signed the Wright Amendment compromise. Shown here are, from left to right, Southwest Airlines' Herb Kelleher, Dallas mayor Laura Miller, Fort Worth mayor Mike Moncrief, American Airlines vice president Dan Garton, and D/FW CEO Jeff Fegan. The compromise phased out the Wright Amendment restrictions on nonstop flights out of Love Field by 2014 while limiting Southwest to 16 gates at the airport. (D/FW.)

Just as there were those who thought the two cities would never agree on a common airport, some believed the scene shown here would never take place. At the Wright Amendment Compromise signing ceremony, Southwest cofounder and chairman Herb Kelleher (left) shakes hands with Kevin Cox, D/FW chief operating officer. Cox's Wright Amendment knowledge and his skills as a negotiator were instrumental in the success of the compromise. (D/FW.)

Volunteers for the Welcome Home a Hero program began greeting US troops on a regular basis in 2004 as they passed through D/FW on their way home for two weeks of rest and recuperation from duty in Kuwait, Iraq, and Afghanistan. After a successful trial the previous year, the North Texas Commission worked with the airport to mobilize greeting groups from nearby cities, chambers of commerce, schools, clubs, and Scout troops. (D/FW.)

The Welcome Home a Hero program at D/FW became so popular that a waiting list had to be created for community groups wanting to participate. Over the life of the program, volunteers greeted more than 460,000 inbound soldiers. The last flight, on March 14, 2012, was greeted with the traditional water cannon salute from the airport's Department of Public Safety. (D/FW.)

Founders Plaza, located on a 20-foot-high berm on the northwest corner of the airport, allows a panoramic view of the airport and its flight operations. It features a granite monument honoring D/FW's founding planners, shade pavilions, sculptures, and speakers relaying real-time radio transmissions between aircraft and the control tower. A memorial to Delta Flight 191 was dedicated in 2012. The plaza is also the location of the airport's official aviation beacon (left), whose rotating green and white lights are on during instrument flight conditions and hours of darkness. The three children of Dennis Smith's sculpture *Share the Dream* (below) pretend to fly while, in the background, British Airways Flight 193 from London's Heathrow Airport is about to touch down on runway 18R on March 13, 2013. (Both, author.)

Eight

D/FW Today

With seven runways, five terminals, and 155 gates, Dallas/Fort Worth International Airport is the highest-capacity airport in the world. No other airport on the globe currently has three control towers and the capability to accommodate four simultaneous landing operations under instrument flying conditions. Today, the airport operations are characterized by even more growth, as new airlines begin service and the airport facilities expand to meet the demand.

Among the new airlines initiating service at D/FW are Virgin America (December 2010), Spirit Airlines (May 2011), Qantas (May 2011), Emirates (February 2012), JetBlue (May 2012), Cayman Airways (June 2012), and WestJet (April 2013). With the advent of JetBlue service, the airport became host to all major US low-cost carriers except Southwest Airlines.

The arrival of Virgin America in particular underscored D/FW's value to the Dallas–Fort Worth Metroplex as an economic engine. The airline decided to come to D/FW because it was the fourth-largest corporate market in the United States. This ranking was largely a result of the number of corporations establishing a presence in the area specifically because of the airport.

In keeping with D/FW's concept of customer-focused growth, the airport in May 2011 embarked on an extensive Terminal Renewal and Improvement Program to upgrade and improve the four original terminals, which had been designed and built before airline deregulation and strict security measures. Although earlier modifications provided increased security while maintaining the efficiency of the semicircular design, the new program also incorporated improved passenger service in ticketing and concession areas.

As outlined in an October 2012 speech by D/FW executive vice president Phil Ritter, the facility's growth is made possible by two great assets: its "land endowment," a legacy of the original planners' foresight in acquiring a large tract of land for the airport; and its airspace, away from the congested air routes that characterize America's coastlines.

On December 1, 2010, low-cost carrier Virgin America inaugurated service at D/FW, the first time that the airline began serving an inland port. According to CEO David Cush, the airline's business model is to attract corporate passengers, and it made sense to come to the Dallas–Fort Worth Metroplex, the fourth-largest corporate market in the nation. In 2011, the airline named one of its Airbus A320 aircraft *dfw one* (shown here). (D/FW.)

Attired in Western regalia, the ever-flamboyant Sir Richard Branson came for the inauguration of D/FW service by Virgin America, one of over 400 companies of his multinational conglomerate Virgin Group. Standing near a temporary corral of Texas longhorns brought to the airport for the occasion, Branson exclaimed to the crowd, "Virgin America is here! You don't have to fly like cattle!" (D/FW.)

On February 2, 2012, Emirates, the largest air carrier in the Middle East, initiated daily nonstop service from D/FW to Dubai, the largest city in the United Arab Emirates. The 8,000-mile trip was scheduled for 14.5 hours to Dubai and 16 hours for the return trip. The difference is due to the usual prevailing westerly winds at altitude. (D/FW.)

The flight to Dubai is not the longest-distance nonstop scheduled into D/FW; that distinction is claimed by Australia's Qantas. On May 17, 2011, Qantas began service to D/FW from Sydney, a 8,566-mile trip. Return flights include a stop at Brisbane due to prevailing winds at altitude. (D/FW.)

The airport's recently renovated Fire Training Research Center is one of the world's most advanced training facilities for airport fire and rescue operations. Crews from several states and foreign countries have trained at the center. Computer-generated graphics allow classroom instructors to project their home airports on large display screens while going through simulated emergency situations. Outside, firefighters get realistic training in mock-ups of passenger and cargo planes as well as a control tower and other structures. The center's Airbus 380 mock-up (below), while shorter than the real aircraft, has the same height and width dimensions and interior configuration. (Both, author.)

No less important to public safety at D/FW is its law enforcement arm. Here, officers conduct an anti-hijacking exercise. Officers receive training in anti-terrorism, negotiations, and SWAT tactics with US military Special Forces and also in countries such as Israel, Spain, Germany, and with England's famed Scotland Yard. The airport police SWAT team is recognized as a leading authority on aircraft assault and hostage rescue procedures. (Alvy Dodson.)

Southwest Airlines announced the purchase of AirTran on September 11, 2010, an acquisition that dictated an end to AirTran flights out of D/FW. One provision of the 2006 Wright Amendment Compromise requires Southwest to surrender one gate at Love Field for every gate that it or an affiliate serves at D/FW. AirTran ceased operations at D/FW on November 21, 2011. (D/FW.)

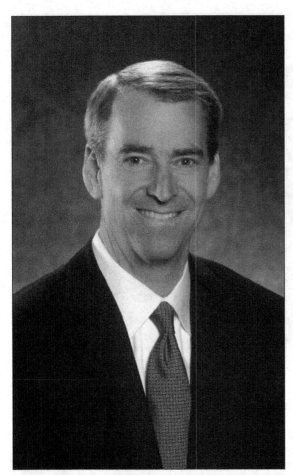

On November 29, 2011, American Airlines filed for Chapter 11 bankruptcy. That day, American's president, Tom Horton (shown here), assumed the additional roles of chairman and CEO, succeeding Gerard Arpey, who elected to retire rather than guide the company through the reorganization process. The announcement carried significant implications for D/FW, since American was its largest tenant, accounting for over 80 percent of the airport's flight operations. (American Airlines.)

When American Airlines filed for Chapter 11 reorganization, US Airways CEO Doug Parker began a campaign to merge his airline with American. (Parker and Tom Horton began their airline careers together at American in the mid-1980s.) At a well-attended press conference at D/FW on February 14, 2013, Horton (right) and Parker announced the proposed merger. The American Airlines name was to be retained. Parker would become CEO and Horton was to be named non-executive chairman. (American Airlines.)

When American Airlines filed for bankruptcy, CEO Tom Horton insisted that any merger action should wait until American emerged from bankruptcy. However, Doug Parker pursued his merger agenda and gained the support of American's labor unions to effect the merger. If finalized, the merger would make D/FW-based American the largest airline in the world. (American Airlines.)

The most unusual aircraft to land at D/FW during its history is unquestionably the Solar Impulse, a solar-powered, long-distance aircraft that arrived in the early morning of May 23, 2013. The aircraft was making a six-stop transcontinental flight to promote renewable energies and new technologies. It was flown alternately by Swiss aviators Bertrand Piccard and Andre Borschberg. The team hopes to fly a similar aircraft nonstop around the world in 2015. (Jay Miller.)

In May 2011, D/FW initiated a $1.9 billion Terminal Renewal and Improvement Program (TRIP) for the four older terminals (A, B, C, and E). In addition to upgrading electrical, plumbing, and other infrastructure systems, TRIP will provide enhanced passenger services, such as improved ticketing and check-in areas (above). Beyond completion of TRIP, the airport looks to the future. Terminal D, the international terminal, is approaching its maximum capacity with increasing operations by both domestic and international airlines. Plans include accommodating more wide-body jets as well as the Airbus A380. Future considerations include the airport's next terminal—Terminal F (below at lower right), south of Terminal D on the west side of International Parkway. The diagram also shows "stingers" projecting from the other terminals to increase their capacity. (Both, D/FW.)

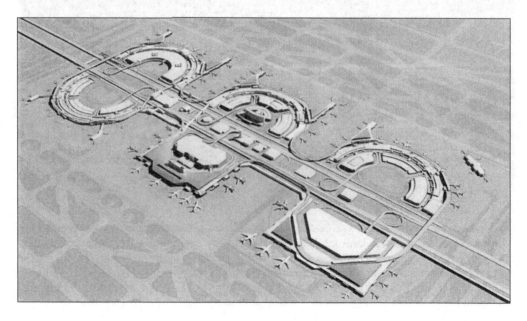

Jeff Fegan, the airport's CEO for virtually the last half of its operational existence, announced his retirement effective September 2013. Named executive director in 1994, Fegan was widely credited with continuing the airport's development as a significant economic engine for North Texas through his philosophy that "the airport is in the economic development business" in addition to being an aviation facility. During his tenure, Fegan directed the $2.7 billion capital development plan, which included construction of International Terminal D, the Skylink people mover system, and the Grand Hyatt D/FW. More recently, he initiated the $1.9 billion Terminal Renewal and Improvement Program to modernize D/FW's four older terminals. Among other capital projects, he also supervised construction of the consolidated Rental Car Center, the International Cargo Centre, Founders Plaza, and the Fire Training Research Center. In addition to massive infrastructure projects, Fegan built successful performance teams that drove the airport's reputation for excellence. His people-oriented approach to "customer-focused growth" has resulted in D/FW's consistent rating among the top five airports in the world for customer service. (D/FW.)

BIBLIOGRAPHY

Bilstein, Roger and Jay Miller. *Aviation in Texas*. Austin: Texas Monthly Press, 1985.

Dallas/Fort Worth International Airport Annual Report, 1998. D/FW International Airport, TX, 1999.

Dallas Morning News. Numerous articles, January 1911–May 2013.

Davies, R.E.G. *Airlines of the United States Since 1914*. Washington, DC: Smithsonian Institution Press, 1998.

Ebinger, Ginger. *The World Connected: DFW International Airport Taking Flight into the 21st Century*. McKinney, TX: DSA Publishing and Design, Inc., 2007.

Fort Worth Star-Telegram. Numerous articles, May 1925–May 2013.

"Just How Big is Dallas/Fort Worth International?" *Smithsonian* (April 1993): 34–47.

NTX: A Profile of the Dallas–Fort Worth Region. D/FW Airport: North Texas Commission, Vol. I, 2012.

Payne, Darwin and Kathy Fitzpatrick. *From Prairie to Planes*. Dallas: Three Forks Press, 1999.

"Southern Prospects," *Airports International*. June 1999: 46–48.

ABOUT THE ORGANIZATIONS

THE FRONTIERS OF FLIGHT MUSEUM

The Frontiers of Flight Museum is located at 6911 Lemmon Avenue, Dallas, Texas, 75209, at the southeast corner of Dallas Love Field Airport. Over 30 aircraft and space vehicles are displayed, including the command module from the *Apollo VII* space mission, the one-of-a-kind Vought V-173 "Flying Pancake," and a complete Southwest Airlines Boeing 737. The museum also holds thousands of rare aviation artifacts, photographs, and memorabilia. Comprehensive public programs for all ages support the museum's position as a community resource to educate, motivate, and inspire the next generation in the disciplines of science, technology, engineering, and mathematics. Hours of operation are 10:00 a.m. to 5:00 p.m., Monday through Saturday and 1:00 to 5:00 p.m. on Sunday. For more information, call 214-350-1651 or visit www.flightmuseum.com.

THE HISTORY OF AVIATION COLLECTION

The University of Texas at Dallas is home to the History of Aviation Collection (HAC), a remarkably extensive resource of aeronautical history. The HAC was founded with the donation of the extensive collection of Dallas aviation journalist George E. Haddaway. Located in the Eugene McDermott Library in the Special Collections Department, the core of the HAC consists of several large collections, including those of airship pioneer Adm. Charles E. Rosendahl and Medal of Honor recipient Gen. James H. "Jimmy" Doolittle, architect of the Doolittle Tokyo Raid. In addition, the HAC also holds several hundred smaller individual collections and an archive of over 50,000 books, journals, and periodicals.

Visit us at
arcadiapublishing.com
···

CPSIA information can be obtained
at www.ICGtesting.com
Printed in the USA
LVOW04*1555080217
523623LV00016B/319/P